D1548569

*A GUIDE TO SPANISH FROM ARGENTINA*

LANGUAGE BABEL, INC.

ISBN: 978-0-692-00502-6

# Other books in the Speaking Latino Series:

- Speaking Boricua

- Speaking Phrases Boricua

- Speaking Chileno

# Table of Contents

## ENGLISH

Table of Contents . . . . . . . . . . . . . . . . . . . . . . . . . . . . . . . 5
Introduction . . . . . . . . . . . . . . . . . . . . . . . . . . . . . . . . . . . 1
Acknowledgements . . . . . . . . . . . . . . . . . . . . . . . . . . . . . . 3
How to Use this Guide . . . . . . . . . . . . . . . . . . . . . . . . . . . . 5
Speak Like an Argentine . . . . . . . . . . . . . . . . . . . . . . . . . . 7
Grammar . . . . . . . . . . . . . . . . . . . . . . . . . . . . . . . . . . . . . . 9
Pronunciation . . . . . . . . . . . . . . . . . . . . . . . . . . . . . . . . . 11
Gestures . . . . . . . . . . . . . . . . . . . . . . . . . . . . . . . . . . . . . 13

## ESPAÑOL

Introducción . . . . . . . . . . . . . . . . . . . . . . . . . . . . . . . . . . 17
Agradecimientos . . . . . . . . . . . . . . . . . . . . . . . . . . . . . . . 19
Cómo usar esta guía . . . . . . . . . . . . . . . . . . . . . . . . . . . . . 21
Hablar como un argentino . . . . . . . . . . . . . . . . . . . . . . . . 23
Gramática . . . . . . . . . . . . . . . . . . . . . . . . . . . . . . . . . . . . 25
Pronunciación . . . . . . . . . . . . . . . . . . . . . . . . . . . . . . . . . 27
Gestos . . . . . . . . . . . . . . . . . . . . . . . . . . . . . . . . . . . . . . . 29

## LEXICON

LEXICON . . . . . . . . . . . . . . . . . . . . . . . . . . . . . . . . . . . . . 33

## ABOUT THE AUTHOR

ABOUT THE AUTHOR . . . . . . . . . . . . . . . . . . . . 111

## QUICK VOCABULARY GUIDES

THE HUMAN BODY . . . . . . . . . . . . . . . . . . . . . . . . . . . . 38
MATE . . . . . . . . . . . . . . . . . . . . . . . . . . . . . . . . . . . . . . . 39
UPSIDE DOWN . . . . . . . . . . . . . . . . . . . . . . . . . . . . . . . 48
CLOTHING . . . . . . . . . . . . . . . . . . . . . . . . . . . . . . . . . . . 55
ALCOHOL . . . . . . . . . . . . . . . . . . . . . . . . . . . . . . . . . . . 65
PEDO . . . . . . . . . . . . . . . . . . . . . . . . . . . . . . . . . . . . . . . 71
FOOD . . . . . . . . . . . . . . . . . . . . . . . . . . . . . . . . . . . . . . . 89
MONEY . . . . . . . . . . . . . . . . . . . . . . . . . . . . . . . . . . . . 100
CRIME . . . . . . . . . . . . . . . . . . . . . . . . . . . . . . . . . . . . . 107

# Introduction

**M**y first kiss from a guy (cheek to cheek, not lip to lip) froze me in place. I mean, I'd never been that close to another guy before, romantically speaking. The aroma of cigarette smoke overwhelmed his clothes, his smoke-stained teeth stuck out and the stubble on his cheek scratched my face. And did I mention? It was guy!

An awkward introduction to Argentina? Not at all! Just a typical gesture of Argentine warmth, emotion and passion, all of which radiate throughout the culture.

Eight years later I still find amusement in the language and expressions of Argentina whenever I visit. I remember sitting in a meeting one day, where eight of us were trying to make a decision about the business. On one end of the table, two people yelled at each other in disagreement. At the other end, another three debated heatedly as well. Another sat in the middle, trying to participate in both debates. Our boss didn't quite know what to do (new to Argentina as well), and I smiled as it dawned on me that I was seeing Argentine passion in action. Everything from the screaming voices, gesticulations and stares in that meeting personify the open emotion seen and heard in Argentina.

This emotion contributes to the fun you will experience learning Argentine Spanish. When an Argentine speaks to you, not only do you hear what he/she thinks, you feel it as well. Gestures, voice patterns and emotions clearly communicate their feelings, whether contempt, annoyance or pleasure. Learn from this passion.

Jared

# Acknowledgements

**F**rom the soothing beach in Ocean Park (Puerto Rico) to the asados and Malbecs of Capital Federal, I'm not sure anyone who worked with me on this thought it would end. A year's hiatus and then another six-month delay stretched the project to several years. Three people spent innumerable hours with me, working on the content, ensuring that I captured the nuances of the language.

Pedro Corradini and his wife, Graciela, sat with me on the beach for hours, working our way through words and definitions. In a nod to the regional differences even within a country, we ran across several words whose meanings the two of them discussed and argued, Pedro being from Buenos Aires and Graciela, Córdoba. Frankly, their heated debates were comical. Both were indispensable to me.

For the second time, Mercedes López Tarnassi (mmlopeztarnassi@gmail.com) has translated the beginning sections into Spanish wonderfully, capturing concisely my ideas. Even more importantly, the three weeks of her intense focus in 2008 proved to be the major push I needed to move this forward. I know she had not planned to spend her vacation slaving over this book with 10-hour days. She is the one person that has helped me throughout the whole process.

Without each of the three of them, I would never have finished this book.

I'd also like to thank Valerie Laigle and Connie Burgwardt for their immense contribution to the nasty words here. I learned more about sexual terms, cussing, insults and just plain bad mouthing then I could have ever expected. How two beautiful women learned those terms, I'd rather not explore. Because of them, this book is much more colorful. Thank you.

Yet again, Diana Caballero helped me finalize the book. She is an amazing woman.

Jared

# How to Use this Guide

To begin, I start with what this book is not. It is not an all-inclusive dictionary. Nor is there any academic basis for what appears here. It is also not a dictionary about *lunfardo* (although you will run across *lunfardo* terms that have entered into daily language). It is a book on slang. Also, the title is NOT a typo. The word Argento is slang for Argentino.

Please also take into account as you read through the guide that the focus of the book is Argentine Spanish from Buenos Aires. While there are terms from other areas as well, the majority of what you see here comes from the capital city. This does not mean that the terms are not the same or will not be understood elsewhere. Just that you will run into other regional usages, meanings and words once you get outside of Buenos Aires that are not documented here. I would appreciate hearing about these as you run across them to include them in the future.

Words are written as close to their grammatically correct spellings as possible. This is not always easy or clear, given that the same word may be commonly spelled more than one way, pronounced several ways or may drop some letters in the pronunciation. For instance, you may run across the spelling *chamullo* and *chamuyo*. These are alternate spellings of the same word. Keep this in mind as you search for words in the guide.

The following symbols appear throughout the book. They will help you along in the learning process.

★      Common word - the most common words you will run into

💣      Dangerous word - these are insulting, naughty, crude or rude words

$      Money - words related to money or finance

[11]      Food and Drink - self explanatory

Sample Entry:

★ **boludez:** 1) trivial, not a big deal. *Te compré un regalito. Es una boludez pero creo que te va a gustar.* 2) something easy, simple that anyone can do. *El examen era una* **boludez**, *me saqué un 10. SYN:* gansada, huevada.

The word entries follow a basic format. First, if applicable, you will see an icon symbol, for instance the ★ above that refers to at least one of the meanings of the entry. Next comes the actual word. Following this are the definitions, with each meaning numbered and separated. Whenever possible, a sample sentence or conversation, to better clarify the word's usage appears in *italics*. Also, note that the word or its form appears in **bold** within the sample phrase. As in the sample above, when a word has more than one definition, each definition and sample phrase will be numbered separately. At the end of the definition, whenever available, the section "*SYN:*" will list any synonyms to the word.

Finally, I use the word Argentine throughout the book instead of Argentinian. I just happen to like it better. They mean the same.

# Speak Like an Argentine

**B**elieve it or not, Argentine is one of the easiest Spanish dialects to identify. Even if you do not understand any of what is said, the pronunciation and rhythms of the language are so distinct you should quickly learn to identify a speaker as a native Argentine. This also means that it should be easy to mimic.

Why would you want to mimic the Argentine accent? I can name several reasons (you decide if they're stupid reasons). The most important and perhaps obvious is to communicate better. You will quickly learn (as with other languages) the same word may take on vastly different meanings with only a change in intonation. When the word *boludo* is pronounced as in bolUUUUUUdo, you can bet that there is some anger or frustration in the speaker's sentence. However, a curt spitting out of *boludo* may just be a term of endearment used between friends (generally guys).

There's also the challenge involved in learning a culture enough to mimic it, or at least to fit in. It feels quite good when your Spanish is fluent enough that someone doesn't recognize where you're from, or that you're not a native speaker.

Another reason is that it is a good icebreaker when you want to meet people or make someone laugh. It's always entertaining to hear a foreigner use typical slang phrases, words and pronunciation in unexpected situations. Walk up to an Argentine friend and say *"Ché, boludo, ¿que hacés acá?"* For added laughter, throw in gesture #2 (in the gesture section) at the same time. Your friend will fall over laughing.

There are 4 major components in learning to speak like a local:
1. Vocabulary
2. Grammar
3. Pronunciation
4. Intonation

Vocabulary is perhaps the most time consuming. To minimize the time, focus on **Speaking Argento's** vocabulary insets and common Argentine words (marked with the symbol ★). Also, listen to conversations, pulling out common phrases. With these tools, you should quickly be improving your local vocabulary.

Grammar really is not that bad. In fact, after a few weeks of local exposure you will be copying common Argentine sentence structures, verb conjugations and similar stuff. This section gives you a couple basic components to review as you prepare your life blending in. But please don't spend much time here. It's better spent out in the street, conversing.

With Pronunciation, again there's really not a lot to cover. Follow the few simple guidelines that appear in this section and you'll be accused of having a local accent in no time.

In my opinion, the hardest of the four areas is to consistently mimic the intonation of a language. This requires lots and lots of practice (at least for me). See the *boludo* example in the second paragraph above for an example of how a word's intonation may change its meaning. Since Argentine is distinct from other Spanish accents in it's intonations you will be able to absorb the local nuances almost effortlessly.

# Grammar

As with other local Spanish languages, Argentine Spanish includes some deviations from typical Spanish grammar. These rules will help you begin to better understand Argentine.

## 1. *Vos:*

In Argentina, the *tu* form of verbs is not used. Instead, *vos* is the term that is used to mean "you." For instance, instead of the typical Spanish phrase *Tu tienes que comprar el pan.* in Argentina the phrase would be *Vos tenés que comprar el pan.*

Verb conjugations for Tú and Vos
Conjugating verbs using the *vos* form is actually easy. Regular verbs adhere to the following scheme:

|  | -AR | -ER | -IR |
|---|---|---|---|
| Tú Conjugation | *tú llamas* | *tú haces* | *tú partes* |
| Vos Conjugation | *vos llamás* | *vos hacés* | *vos partís* |

Irregular verbs can be a bit different, but since each one is unique you will have to learn them on the fly. A couple irregular verbs are *decir* and *venir.*

## 2. *Acordarse / recordar:*

The word *acordarse* is commonly used instead of the grammatically correct word recordar. An example is the sentence *Me acuerdo que hablamos de eso la semana pasada.* The correct version would be *Recuerdo que hablamos de eso la semana pasada.*

## 3. *re-:*

The prefix *re-* for any word demonstrates "extra" of whatever is said. For example, *re-canchero* would mean extremely cool, nifty or neat. The sentence *Martín se vistió re-canchero para salir con María* would mean that *Martín dressed extremely snazzy (or cool) to go out with María.*

# Pronunciation

**H**ere are a few Argentine sounds that you will quickly recognize once in Argentina. Please keep in mind that pronunciation hints in this section are based on English sounds. Also, different social classes have different pronunciations, so you should listen for this as well.

1. *Y is ZH or SH sound*
   The letter Y is often pronounced similar to the S sound in *vision* (in other words a ZH sound). In some social classes it may be pronounced as an SH sound, especially in Buenos Aires. This is becoming a more common pronunciation than in the past.

2. *LL is ZH or SH sound*
   This is the exact same as #1 above.

3. *Drop the letters D and S from the end of a word*
   It is typical to drop the letters D and S when they end a sentence. For instance, the sentence "*Es verdad.*" would be pronounced more like "*E verdá.*"

4. *S is more of an H sound*
   The letter S may be pronounced more silently as if it were an English H, as in the word HAT. The word *mosca* would become *mohca.*

# Gestures

**A** major part of fitting in with Argentines, as I mentioned in the **Introduction**, is their passion. Gestures and body language in Argentina are an obligatory part of communication. Even without speaking a word, with these gestures you will clearly communicate your thoughts to the locals.

Here are examples that within a few days of being in Argentina you will begin to see and copy. Unfortunately, they are not always possible to describe clearly in writing. Ask someone to show you how to use them properly.

## 1. <u>Aportar</u>

**Gesture:** Thumb over finger with fist touching a surface

**Meaning:** Put in money or invest, financed by, paid off

For this gesture, close your four fingers over your palm, making sure the fingertips point straight back towards the inside of your elbow. The thumb should be on top of the already closed index finger facing away from your body. Next, moving your fist at the wrist only (keep the arm still) swing your fist down, maintaining your arm parallel to the ground. Then, with the flat surface area formed between your knuckles and first joints on the four fingers, lock your wrist and touch or hit a table, or similar surface. It is also common to hit the palm of your other hand, instead of a hard surface.

## 2. ¿Qué es esto?

**Gesture:** fingertips touching, facing upwards

**Meaning:** means "what was that all about", "what was he thinking?", "what's going on"

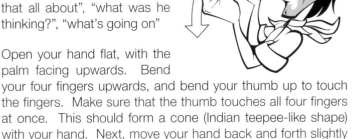

Open your hand flat, with the palm facing upwards. Bend your four fingers upwards, and bend your thumb up to touch the fingers. Make sure that the thumb touches all four fingers at once. This should form a cone (Indian teepee-like shape) with your hand. Next, move your hand back and forth slightly at the wrist two or three times. It is also common to make the gesture with both hands at once.

## 3. Prolijo

**Gesture:** fingers towards body hand in line moves downward

**Meaning:** well-mannered, serious, respectful, a correct person

Touch your thumb to your index finger on your right hand. Make sure that each finger touches the finger(s) next to it. Place your hand, with fingers pointing to your chest, touching the middle of your chest about 2 inches below your neck. Slowly move your hand down your chest, as if tracing a tie that hangs down. Your hand should drop about 3-4 inches in the process.

## 4. <u>Andá (a cagar)</u>

**Gesture:** hand open facing body, arm moves from lower position upward

**Meaning:** screw off, get the hell out of here

Hold your right palm open, facing your body, directly in front of your chest. Without moving your elbow, rapidly move your hand towards the right, so your hand points directly up towards the sky.

## 5. <u>¡Ojo!</u>

**Gesture:** Finger pulls down lower part of eye

**Meaning:** Keep your eyes open for crooks or being ripped off, be careful about something

Using your right index finger, lightly pull down the lower part of your right eye by curling your finger. At the same time, turn your head slightly down and to the right. This may also be used with the left eye, by reversing the directions (any time the word right appears above replace with the word left) of each step.

## 6. <u>Hace tiempo / Falta mucho</u>

**Gesture:** vertical hand back and forth

**Meaning:** 1) a long time ago,  2) keep going for a while longer, you still have a ways to go

Place your hand, palm open facing toward your ear.  Leave two inches between your ear and palm.  For the first gesture (1), move your hand backward at the wrist, then forward a couple times.  For gesture two (2), move your hand forward at the wrist, and then backward a couple times.  Both are similar to the action of throwing (or pump-faking) an American football.

• Meaning 1 •          • Meaning 2 •

# Introducción

**L**a primera vez que un tipo me dio un beso (en el cachete, no en la boca) me quedé helado. Es decir, nunca en mi vida había estado tan cerca de otro hombre en términos amorosos. El aroma a cigarrillo en su ropa era abrumador. Tenía los dientes amarillentos y la barba de tres días me raspaba la cara. ¿Ya les aclaré que era un tipo?

¿Les parece una presentación poco elegante de la Argentina? Al contrario. Es sólo un gesto típico de la calidez, el sentimiento y la pasión que irradia su cultura.

Ocho años más tarde, cada vez que voy a Argentina, siguen pareciéndome divertidos el lenguaje y las expresiones que se usan en este país. Me acuerdo que un día estaba en una reunión de ocho personas tratando de tomar decisiones con respecto al negocio. En un extremo de la mesa había dos personas a los gritos en total desacuerdo. En el otro extremo había otras tres que también sostenían un debate candente. Otra persona sentada entre los dos bandos trataba de participar en ambos debates. Nuestro jefe no sabía muy bien qué hacer (también recién llegado a Argentina) y a mí se me dibujó una sonrisa en la cara cuando caí en la cuenta de que estaba en presencia de la pasión argentina en acción. Absolutamente todo, desde las voces gritonas, las gesticulaciones y las miradas fijas que pude apreciar en esa reunión personificaban el sentimiento a flor de piel que se observa y se escucha en Argentina.

Este sentimiento a flor de piel les va a resultar muy divertido cuando aprendan a hablar el español de Argentina. Cuando te habla un argentino, no sólo escuchás lo que piensa sino que a la vez, lo sentís en carne propia. Los gestos, los patrones de voz y las emociones transmiten claramente sus sentimientos, ya sea de desprecio, enojo o placer. Aprendé sobre esta pasión.

Jared

# Agradecimientos

**D**esde los escenarios de las relajantes playas de Ocean Park (Puerto Rico) hasta los asados y vinos Malbec en la Capital Federal, no creo que ninguno de los que trabajaron conmigo en este proyecto haya pensado que alguna vez se iba a terminar. Hice un paréntesis de un año y después hubo seis meses de atraso que hicieron que el proyecto tardara varios años. Hubo tres personas que pasaron incontables horas conmigo trabajando sobre el contenido del libro para ver si yo había capturado bien los matices del idioma.

Pedro Corradini y su mujer, Graciela, pasaron muchísimas horas conmigo sentados en la playa trabajando sobre las palabras y sus definiciones. Haciendo eco de las diferencias regionales incluso dentro de un mismo país, nos encontramos con palabras que generaban discusiones y hasta peleas entre ellos en torno a su significado, ya que Pedro es de Buenos Aires y Graciela, de Córdoba. Sinceramente, sus discusiones candentes me daban risa. Los dos fueron indispensables para escribir este libro.

Por segunda vez, Mercedes López Tarnassi (mmlopeztarnassi@gmail.com) hizo las traducciones al español de las secciones introductorias y logró reflejar mis ideas de manera concisa. Lo más importante además de eso fue que nuestras tres semanas de trabajo intenso en 2008 terminaron siendo el gran empujón que necesitaba para seguir adelante con el proyecto. Sé muy bien que no estaba en sus planes pasar sus vacaciones invirtiendo arduas jornadas de 10 horas en este libro. Fue la persona que me ayudó a lo largo de todo el proceso.

Sin la participación de ellos tres, nunca hubiera terminado este libro.

También quiero agradecer a Valerie Laigle y Connie Burgwardt por su inmenso aporte a la lista de malas palabras. Aprendí más términos sexuales, groserías, insultos y formas de despotricar de lo que me hubiera imaginado. Más vale que no me ponga a averiguar cómo dos mujeres tan lindas aprendieron a decir semejantes cosas. Gracias a ellas, este libro es mucho más colorido. Les agradezco su colaboración.

Nuevamente, gracias a Diana Caballero que me ayudó a terminar el libro. Es una mujer espectacular.

Jared

# Cómo Usar Esta Guía

**V**oy a empezar por contarles de qué no se trata este libro. No es un diccionario enciclopédico y su contenido no tiene sustento académico. Tampoco es un diccionario de lunfardo (aunque sí van a encontrar términos lunfardos que se han incorporado al lenguaje cotidiano). Se trata de un libro de modismos. Fíjense que el título no es un error tipográfico. La palabra Argento es un modismo local que significa Argentino.

Tengan en cuenta, además, que esta guía se concentra básicamente en el español argentino de Buenos Aires. Si bien incluye palabras de otras regiones también, la mayoría proviene de la ciudad capital, lo que no significa que no sean iguales o no vayan a ser captadas en otros lados. Sólo quiere decir que se van a encontrar con distintos usos, significados y términos regionales cuando trasciendan los límites de Buenos Aires que no están documentados en esta guía. Les voy a agradecer que me hagan llegar sus comentarios cuando se encuentren con alguna palabra de este tipo para poder incluirlas en futuros trabajos.

Las palabras están escritas con la mayor aproximación posible a su forma gramaticalmente correcta. No siempre es tan fácil o queda tan claro ya que a veces el mismo término se escribe de más de una forma, se pronuncia de varias distintas y hasta puede haber letras que no se pronuncien. Por ejemplo, van a ver escrito *chamuyo* o *chamullo*. Cada ejemplo ilustra formas alternativas de escribir la misma palabra. Tengan esto en cuenta cuando busquen términos en esta guía.

Los siguientes símbolos aparecen en todo el libro y van a ayudarlos en este proceso de aprendizaje.

★   Palabras comunes - las palabras más frecuentes con las que van a encontrarse

💣   Palabras peligrosas - son insultos o malas palabras, groserías o términos ofensivos

$   Dinero - estas palabras están relacionadas con el dinero y las finanzas

🍴   Comida– no hace falta explicación

Ejemplo:

★ **boludez:** 1) trivial, not a big deal. *Te compré un regalito. Es una boludez pero creo que te va a gustar.* 2) something easy, simple that anyone can do. *El examen era una boludez, me saqué un 10.* SYN: gansada, huevada.

Las entradas siguen un formato básico. En los casos que corresponda, primero van a ver un símbolo (por ejemplo la ★ en el ejemplo) que se refiere a por lo menos uno de los significados de la palabra o frase.

Después aparece el término y luego las definiciones. Cada significado se encuentra numerado y explicado por separado. En algunos casos, hay una oración o diálogo en cursiva a modo de ejemplo para ilustrar de manera más clara el uso de las palabras y dentro de los ejemplos, éstas se encuentran resaltadas en **negrita**. Como con los ejemplos, cuando una palabra tiene más de una definición, cada una de ellas y sus ejemplos están numerados por separado. Al final, la sección "SYN" incluye los sinónimos, si los hay.

Finalmente, usé la palabra "Argentine" y no "Argentinian" en todo el libro pero sólo porque me gusta más. Significan exactamente lo mismo.

# Hablar Como Un Argentino

Aunque no lo crean, el argentino es uno de los dialectos españoles más fáciles de identificar. Incluso para los que no entienden ni una palabra, como la pronunciación y los ritmos del idioma son tan distintivos, enseguida pueden aprender a identificar cuando un hispanoparlante es argentino. Esto además se refleja en lo fácil que puede ser imitarlos.

¿Para qué alguien querría imitar el acento argentino? Les puedo enumerar varios motivos (ustedes dirán si son estupideces). El más importante y quizás más obvio es para comunicarse mejor. En seguida van a aprender (igual que con otros idiomas) que una misma palabra puede adoptar significados muy diferentes con sólo cambiar la entonación. Si una persona dice la palabra *boludo* arrastrando la U, seguro que está un poco enojada o denota frustración (¡bolUUUUdo!). Sin embargo, en otros contextos decir *boludo* a secas es una expresión de cariño utilizada entre amigos (en general, entre varones).

Otro motivo es el desafío de aprender la cultura a tal punto de poder imitarla o por lo menos, integrarse. Es linda la sensación de hablar español de manera tan fluida que los demás no reconozcan de dónde somos o no se den cuenta de que no es nuestra lengua materna.

También sirve para romper el hielo si quieren conocer gente o hacer reír a alguien. Es divertido escuchar a un extranjero utilizar frases, palabras y pronunciaciones típicas de la jerga local en situaciones imprevistas. Prueben esto. Acérquense a un amigo argentino y díganle: *"Ché, boludo, ¿que hacés acá?"*. Para que se rían todavía más, métanle el gesto N°2 (en la sección gestos). El tipo se va a revolcar de la risa.

En el proceso de aprendizaje, existen 4 componentes principales para hablar como un local:
1.    Vocabulario
2.    Gramática
3.    Pronunciación
4.    Entonación

El vocabulario es quizás la parte que más tiempo lleva. Para hacerlo en el menor tiempo posible, concéntrense en los recuadros de vocabulario y las palabras de uso típico marcadas con el símbolo ★. Además, escuchen conversaciones atentamente para sacar frases de uso común. Con estas herramientas, rápidamente van a aumentar el nivel de localismos.

En cuanto a la gramática, no es tan grave el asunto. De hecho, después de unas semanas de exposición, van a estar copiando la forma argentina de estructurar las oraciones, conjugar los verbos y cosas por el estilo. Esta sección brinda un par de elementos básicos para repasar en el proceso de preparación para integrarse a la cultura. Les aconsejo que no inviertan demasiado tiempo en esto. La mejor inversión es en la calle, conversando con la gente.

Lo mismo pasa con la pronunciación. No hay demasiado para cubrir. Sigan las sencillas pautas incluidas en esta sección y los van a acusar de tener un acento local en muy poco tiempo.

A mi parecer, la más difícil de las cuatro habilidades es la de imitar coherentemente la entonación de un idioma. Esto requiere muchísima práctica (por lo menos en mi caso). Mirá el ejemplo de *boludo* en el segundo párrafo arriba para entender cómo la entonación de una palabra puede cambiar su significado. Como los argentinos tienen una entonación tan particular, van a poder absorber los matices casi sin esfuerzo.

# Gramática

Igual que otros tipos de español local, el español de Argentina sufre algunas desviaciones en la gramática. Estas reglas sirven para entender mejor el argentino.

## 1. *Vos:*

En Argentina no se usa la forma *tu* del verbo sino el pronombre *vos*. Por ejemplo, en lugar de decir *Tú tienes que comprar el pan*, los argentinos dicen *Vos tenés que comprar el pan*.

Conjugación del verbo con Tú y con Vos
Es realmente fácil conjugar los verbos con el pronombre *vos*. Los verbos regulares cumplen con el siguiente patrón:

|                  | -AR        | -ER       | -IR        |
|------------------|------------|-----------|------------|
| Tú Conjugación   | tú llamas  | tú haces  | tú partes  |
| Vos Conjugación  | vos llamás | vos hacés | vos partís |

Los verbos irregulares varían un poco en su forma pero como cada uno de ellos es diferente, los van a tener que aprender sobre la marcha. Un par de verbos irregulares son *decir* y *venir*.

## 2. *Acordarse / recordar:*

El verbo reflexivo *acordarse* es de uso común en lugar de su forma gramaticalmente correcta, *recordar*. Por ejemplo, la oración *Me acuerdo que hablamos de eso la semana pasada*. La versión correcta sería *Recuerdo que hablamos de eso la semana pasada*.

## 3. *re-:*

El prefijo *re-* antepuesto a cualquier palabra significa "más" de lo que se está hablando. Por ejemplo, *re-canchero* quiere decir muy copado, que tiene mucha onda. En la oración *Martín se vistió re-canchero para salir con María*, -re quiere decir que *Martín se vistió muy elegante para salir con María*.

# Pronunciación

**E**n esta sección se describen algunos de los sonidos que en seguida van a reconocer cuando pisen suelo argentino. Tengan en cuenta que las pautas de pronunciación se basan en sonidos del inglés. También tengan presente que la pronunciación de ciertos sonidos varía según el estrato social, así que estén atentos a estas diferencias.

1. *Y se pronuncia ZH o SH*

   La letra Y en general se pronuncia como la S en la palabra *vision* en inglés (ZH). En algunas clases sociales y de manera cada vez más generalizada se pronuncia con el sonido SH, principalmente en la ciudad de Buenos Aires.

2. *LL se pronuncia ZH o SH*

   Lo mismo que en el punto 1.

3. *Las letras D y S no se pronuncian al final de una palabra*

   Es muy común no pronunciar las letras D y S cuando se encuentran al final de una oración. Por ejemplo, la oración "*es verdad*" se transforma en "*e  verdá*".

4. *La S intervocálica adopta el sonido H*

   La letra S en posición intervocálica es más silenciosa, como si fuera el sonido H en inglés, como en la palabra HAT. Por ejemplo, la palabra *mosca* se pronuncia *mohca*.

# Gestos

Una parte importante para integrarse con los argentinos, como mencioné en la introducción, es la pasión. Los gestos y el lenguaje corporal en Argentina son una parte que no puede faltar dentro de la comunicación. Sin decir una sola palabra, con sólo utilizar estos gestos, podrán comunicar claramente sus pensamientos a los locales.

Acá tienen algunos gestos que con sólo algunos días en Argentina, van a empezar a ver y a copiar. Lamentablemente, no siempre es tan fácil describirlos claramente por escrito. Les sugiero que le pidan a alguien que les muestre cómo usarlos correctamente.

## 1. Aportar

**Gesto:** el pulgar sobre los dedos con el puño golpeando una superficie

**Significado:** poner dinero o invertir, financiar, saldar

Para hacer este gesto, cerrar los dedos hacia la palma de la mano con la punta mirando hacia el interior del codo y colocar el pulgar por encima del índice pero apuntando hacia fuera. Después, girar el puño hacia abajo con una flexión de muñeca. El brazo queda quieto, paralelo al piso. Con la superficie formada entre los nudillos y la primera articulación de los dedos, dar un golpe sobre la mesa o una superficie similar sin articular la muñeca. También es común golpear la palma extendida de la otra mano.

## 2. ¿Qué es esto?

**Gesto:** las yemas de los dedos amuchadas mirando hacia arriba

**Significado:** ¿qué pasa? ¿qué fue eso? ¿qué estás diciendo?

Abrir la mano con la palma mirando hacia el techo. Flexionar todos dedos hacia arriba, de manera que el pulgar toque las yemas de los otros cuatro dedos. Así, la mano queda en forma de cono, como si fuera una carpa. Luego, flexionar la muñeca hacia arriba y hacia abajo dos o tres veces. También es común hacer el gesto con las dos manos.

## 3. Prolijo

**Gesto:** los dedos apuntando hacia el cuerpo, la mano se desplaza en línea recta hacia abajo

**Significado:** educado, serio, respetuoso, una persona correcta

Juntar los dedos índice y pulgar de la mano derecha y fíjarse que el resto de los dedos se toquen con el de al lado. Ubicar la mano a la altura del pecho, con los dedos apuntando hacia adentro, unos centímetros por debajo del cuello. Despacio, desplazar la mano hacia abajo en la línea del pecho como si estuvieran siguiendo el recorrido de una corbata. La mano desciende unos 10 centímetros en este proceso.

## 4. Andá (a cagar)

**Gesto:** la mano abierta en dirección al cuerpo, el brazo se desplaza hacia arriba

**Significado:** vete a la mierda.

Poner la mano con la palma extendida mirando hacia usted directamente en frente del pecho, y sin mover el codo, llevar la mano hacia arriba a la derecha con un movimiento rápido de manera que la mano quede apuntando hacia el techo.

## 5. ¡Ojo!

**Gesto:** el índice empuja hacia abajo la parte inferior del ojo

**Significado:** abrí los ojos y fijáte que no te estafen, tené cuidado con lo que sea, ¡Cuidado!

Con el índice de la mano derecha, empujar despacio hacia abajo la parte inferior del ojo. Al mismo tiempo, inclinar la cabeza apenas hacia abajo y un poco a la derecha. También se puede hacer con el ojo izquierdo invirtiendo todas las direcciones en cada paso (reemplazar derecha por izquierda).

## 6. Hace tiempo / Falta mucho

**Gesto:** la mano vertical hacia adelante y hacia atrás

**Significado:** 1) hace mucho tiempo  2) seguí un rato más, todavía falta

Poner la mano con la palma extendida mirando la oreja. Dejar un espacio de 5 centímetros entre la oreja y la palma. Para el gesto (1), mover la mano hacia delante con una flexión de muñeca y luego hacia atrás un par de veces. Para el gesto (2), mover la mano hacia atrás con una flexión de muñeca y luego hacia adelante un par de veces.

Los dos gestos se parecen a la acción de lanzar o hacer de cuenta que se lanza una pelota de fútbol americano.

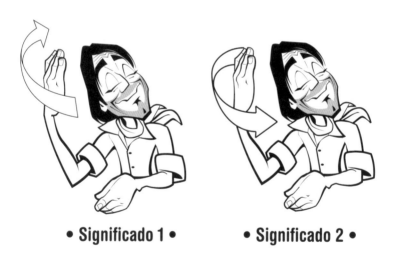

• Significado 1 •          • Significado 2 •

# SPEAKING ARGENTO

## A Guide to Argentine Slang

# LEXICON:

**10 puntos:** to be okay. *¿Cómo te fue en el exámen?* ***10 puntos.*** *SYN:* joya.

★ **a full:** fully occupied, overworked. *Fabián, estoy a full con laburo asi que te llamo más tarde. SYN:* a pleno.

• a los pedos •

**a los pedos:** extremely fast, in a hurry. *Me cambié **a los pedos** porque me estaban esperando en la puerta.*

**a pata:** to be on foot, carless. *¿Vamos **a pata** o tomamos un taxi?*

**¡a pleno!:** Yes!, You bet!, a definite yes.

**a rolete:** a lot of something. *Compramos comida **a rolete** para la fiesta. Sobró más de la mitad. SYN:* una bocha, un vagón.

**a seguro se lo llevaron preso:** you can't take anything for granted, nothing is "for sure".

**a todo lo que da:** at full speed, full steam.

**abatatarse:** to be frozen with fright.

**abombado:** 1) to be dumb–founded due to too much work or hot weather  2) spoiled, for example meat.

**abrir cancha:** to make room or make way for something, for example, a fight.

**abrirse:**  to step out, stop taking part in. *Menem se abrió del desempate electoral. SYN:* bajarse.

**abrochadora:** stapler.

💣 **acabar:** to cum.

🍴 **aceto:** balsamic vinegar, a more common spanish word is *vinagre balsámico*.

**achicar:** to chicken out, lose courage. *No te achiques, vos podés hacerlo. SYN:* arrugar.

**acomodar:** to recommend or influence, to favor. *Entró a la empresa acomodado por su tío, el gerente regional.*

★ **afanar:** to steal, rob or swindle. *SYN:* chorear.

**afilador:** a person that goes door to door sharpening kni-ves.

**aflojar:** 1) to cut down on something. *Aflojá con los postres, estás gordita. / Aflojá con las malas palabras, estás hablando con gente mayor.* 2) to stop being uptight. *Aflojá, ya hace dos semanas que no me hablás.*

**agarrada:** a verbal argument. *Tuve una agarrada con mi jefe ayer. SYN:* encontronazo.

**agarrarse a trompadas:** beat the hell out of.

**agarrárselas:** to pick on someone. *Si tenés un mal día es cosa tuya, no las agarres conmigo.*

**agrandado:** having a big ego, full of yourself. *SYN:* creido, fanfarrón.

★ **aguardar:** to wait a minu-te, to hold on a minute. *Aguár-dame un minuto, que tengo alguien en la otra línea.*

**al cuete:** uselessly. *SYN:* al pedo, al dope, al divino botón.

**al divino botón:** uselessly. *SYN:* al pedo, al dope, al cuete.

**al dope:** farting around, screwing off, not doing any-thing, wasting time, the inverse of *al pedo*.

★ ● **al palo:** 1) to have an erection 2) to be horny. *La secretaria me tiene **al palo** todo el día, está tan buena.*

★ ● **al pedo:** something useless, that didn't need to be done, or that was a waste of time. *Hice todos los trámites **al pedo** porque al final no me otorgaron la beca. SYN:* al cuete, al dope, al divino botón.

**al pelo:** okay, you got it, all clear, you bet. *SYN:* joya, listo, a pleno, a full.

▦ **alcaucil:** artichoke, the more common spanish word is *alcachofa*.

▦ **alfajor:** a cookie-like sweet often made with *dulce de leche* and covered in chocolate, although a variety of types and flavors exists.

**alpargatas:** kind of *gaucho* footwear made of knitted rope, canvas and an elastic opening on the upper side.

**alpedear:** to idle about.

● **alzado:** horny. *SYN:* al palo, en llamas.

$ **amarrete:** cheap, stingy.

*SYN:* codito, rasca, ratón, rata.

$ **amarrocar:** to save money.

**ambiente:** one room in an apartment, either living, dining or bedroom. For example an apartment with 4 *ambientes* will generally have 3 bedrooms and a living room. *Se vende departamento de dos **ambientes**, cocina y baño completos.*

● **amigarche:** a combination of the words *amigo* and *garche*, refers to someone in between a friend and boyfriend, friend with benefits. *SYN:* amigovio, amigo con derecho a roce.

**amigo con derecho a roce:** a friend you occasionally have sex with, friends with benefits. *SYN:* amigovio, amigarche.

**amigovio/a:** a combination of the words *amigo* and *novio*, refers to someone in between a friend and boyfriend, friend with benefits. *SYN:* amigarche, amigo con derecho a.

▦ **ananá:** pineapple, the common spanish word is *piña*.

★ ● **andá a cagar:** literally "go take a shit", buzz off,

# andá a cantarle a Gardel

go fly a kite, screw off (may be used seriously or playfully among friends). *SYN:* andáte a la mierda.

**andá a cantarle a Gardel:** buzz off, go away.

★ **¡Andá!:** 1) Come on! Give me a break! No way! *Me aumentaron el sueldo al doble. ¡Andá!* 2) Get out of here, Who do you think you are? *¡Andá! ¿Quién te crees que sos?*

★ 💣 **andar para el carajo:** bad, wrong, used to express that something works wrongly, somebody feels bad, something was inappropriate. *Este auto **anda para el carajo**, necesito cambiarlo por uno nuevo. / Me siento **para el carajo**. / Creo que estoy por enfermar.Lo trató **para el carajo**, tenía razón en enojarse. SYN:* para el orto.

★ 💣 **aparato:** a real jerk, a tool, an ass. *SYN:* zapallo.

**apretar:** to make out.

**¡Araca!:** Look out! Here come the cops!

**arbolito:** an illegal money changer (the changing of money is controlled by the government).

💣 **argolla:** pussy. *SYN:* chichi, chacón

**armarse la gorda:** to cause a situation, a problem, a conflict. *Si te ve tu madre con esos tatuajes **se arma la gorda**.*

**arrastrar el ala:** to pursue someone romantically, to court someone. *Nena, ¿quién te **arrastra el ala**? ¿algún festejante en la mira? SYN:* festejar.

**arrugar:** to chicken out. *Iba a decirle toda la verdad pero **arrugué** a último momento.*

**aspamento:** an exaggerated demonstration of feelings or emotions. *Dejá de hacer **aspamento** y andá al grano. ¿Qué fue lo que pasó?*

**asustado como perro en bote:** really scared.

**atenti:** Attention! Over here! Look out!

**aterrizar:** literally "to land", to come back to reality.

💣 **atorranta:** a slut or easy woman.

**atorrante:** 1) unemployed, homeless person 2) not trustworthy, shameless, lazy.

**atorrantear:** to laze around, to not do anything, to be a vagrant.

$ **austral:** name of former currency used in Argentina, replaced by the peso in 1992.

**avivada:** do something illegal or improper to take a small advantage. *Es la típica avivada porteña, pagamos el cable a medias con el vecino y nos colgamos.*

**avivarse:** to realize, become aware of. *No me avivé de que estaba a dos cuadras del banco. Podría haber ido a depositar el cheque. SYN: apiolarse.*

**baboso:** a lecherous person. *Es muy buen profesor pero a las mujeres nos incomoda que sea tan baboso.*

**bacán:** wealthy, well off, living the good life. *Tu madre y yo estamos viviendo como bacanes desde que ustedes se casaron m'hijo, nos damos todos los gustos.*

**bacanazo:** refined, well off.

**bagayero:** a man who dates ugly women, thinking they are gorgeous. *¡Sos un bagayero, era la chica más fea del boliche!*

**bagayo:** 1) a little piece of luggage or bag. 2) a clumsy, ugly woman.

**bagre:** ugly girl. *Qué va a tener novio si es un bagre la pobre!*

**bajar un cambio:** literally to shift down a gear, to chill out, cool off or relax. *Bajá un cambio o vas a terminar internado por estrés.*

🍒 **bajarle la caña:** to have sex.

**bajón:** a damper on things, something that depresses your mood. *¡Que bajón! Tuvimos que cancelar el viaje por el clima.*

**baldosa:** a ceramic tile.

**balero:** head.

**¡bancá!:** Wait!

★ **bancar(se):** 1) to finance, to back, to support financially. *¿Me bancás un paquete de cigarrillos?* 2) to put up with, tolerate. *Andáte, no te banco más.* 3) to wait for. *Yo te banco hasta las siete, si no llegás me voy.*

★ **bancar un toque:** Hold on a second! Wait a minute! *Báncame un toque, ya vengo.*

## THE HUMAN BODY

**balero:** head
**bobo:** heart
**bocho:** 1) a smart, intellectual person  2) a head
**bolas:** a guy's balls, nuts
**busarda / buzarda:** stomach or belly
**buzón:** a large mouth
**caripela:** face
**carucha:** face
**chapas:** long hair
**cola:** rear end
**crenchas:** long and messy hair
**croqueta:** head
**cucusa:** head
**cuore:** heart
**gamba:** a leg
**garfios:** fingers
**jamones:** large legs or thighs, for a woman
**jeta:** face
**jetón:** a large-mouthed person or someone with a large face
**marote:** a head
**napia:** nose
**naso:** nose
**ñata:** nose
**sabiola:** a head
**traste:** rear end, heinie

**baranda:** a stench. *¡Qué baranda a mierda!*

★ **bárbaro:** 1) cool, great. *¡Qué bárbaro te quedó el vestido!* 2) a big deal, huge (as in a problem or mess). *Tiene un mambo bárbaro en la cabeza.*

**bardear:** to screw up, mess up. *No la paso bien en la casa de mi novio porque sus hermanas me bardean todo el tiempo. SYN: joder.*

**bardero:** someone that complicates things or screws up stuff. *No quiero que mi hijo se junte con ese porque es muy bardero. SYN: jodón.*

**bardo:** 1) a mess. *Había un bardo en la calle pero nadie sabía qué había pasado. SYN: quilombo.* 2) something difficult to do or understand.

**barra:** 1) a bar.  2) group of friends. *SYN: los pibes.*  3) group of fans, often with a reputation for violence.

**barra brava:** the 12th man (for a sports team, specifically soccer) in reference to the influence that the spectators can have in a game.

**barrilete:** kite, the more common spanish word is *cometa.*

## MATE

*Drinking mate is a ritual for many Argentines. You will see people walking around with thermoses under one arm, and the mate gourd in a hand. Hot water is poured into the gourd, mixing with the bitter mate leaves and then drunk through the straw. Adding sugar to reduce the bitterness is optional. Also, it is quite common to pass the gourd around, sharing among friends.*

**bombilla:** the metal straw used for drinking mate
**cebar:** to serve mate
**cimarrón:** bitter mate
**mate:** 1) a bitter tea that is almost a religious experience for many Argentines, the process of drinking mate is often more social than anything else  2) the special container from which the tea is drunk
**yerba:** the tea that is used in drinking mate
**bizcocho:** oval crackers that accompany *mate*

**bártulos:** things, stuff. *Dejá los bártulos en casa y después pasamos a buscarlos.*

**basurear:** to humiliate. *No entiendo cómo los empleados se dejan basurear por ese tirano.*

**batata:** old car. *SYN:* catramina.

**batidor:** a snitch, informant.

**batifondo:** a mess.

**batir:** to snitch on, say, tell (something one does not know much about, accurate facts, tell a lie, etc.) *SYN:* mandar fruta.

**batir la posta:** to say the exact truth. *Pregúntale al quiosquero que siempre te bate la posta.*

**berreta, berretada:** 1) sleazy, cheap, poor quality  2) a fake object. *SYN:* trucho.

**berretín:** 1) an illusion, a fantasy  2) burning desire.

**biaba:** a beating.

# bicicletear

• bicicletear •

**bicicletear:** to make excuses to not pay money (come back tomorrow). *Estoy corta de guita porque los clientes me vienen **bicicleteando** hace meses.*

**bicicletero:** someone that makes excuses to avoid paying money.

**bienudo:** stuck up, usually because of wealth and social status.

**bife:** a face slap. *SYN:* bofe.

⑪ **bife a caballo:** beef with fried eggs and French Fries.

**billetera mata galán:** money gets you more chicks than good looks, literally "wallet kills a nice looking man". *Se casó con un hombre 15 años mayor y bien feo. Claro, **billetera mata galán.***

★ **birome:** a pen.

⑪ **birra:** a beer.

⑪ **bizcocho:** oval crackers that accompany *mate.*

**blef:** a bluff.

**bobo:** heart. *SYN:* cuore.

**bocasucia:** literally "dirty mouth", someone who says four letter and vulgar words regularly.

**bocha:** a bunch, a lot. *Me dieron una **bocha** de trabajo para el fin de semana. SYN:* vagón.

• billetera mata galán •

**bochinche:** a loud noise, people making noise, usually in the context of a party, a fight, children playing, etc. *Paren el **bochinche** que quiero dormir la siesta. SYN:* quilombo.

**bocho:** 1) a smart, intellectual person. 2) a head. *SYN:* sabiola, marote, croqueta.

**balero:** head.

**bocina:** a snitch.

**bocón:** a snitch.

**bodegón:** a dive bar, a cheap place to drink.

**bofe:** a punch, slap or hit.

**boga:** lawyer.

**bolacear:** to lie, to bullshit, to completely make up. *SYN:* versear, guitarrear.

**bolacero:** a liar. *No le creas nada porque es un **bolacero**.*

✺ **bolas:** 1) a guy's balls, nuts. SYN: pelotas. 2) a short form of *boludo* used to address someone you're talking to. *SYN:* boludo.

**bolas tristes:** a fool, a jerk.

**bolazo:** a huge lie. *Le metí un **bolazo** y se lo re comió.*

*Es un aparato.*

**boleado:** confused, disoriented.

★ **boliche:** a nightclub, a bar. *Anoche estuvimos en el **boliche** hasta las 4 bailando, y después fuimos a tomar un café.*

✺ **bolitas:** insulting term for Bolivians.

**bollo:** a punch, slap or hit. *Me pegó un **bollo** en la jeta que me dejó tarado. SYN:* piña.

**bolu, bolú:** a short form of *boludo*, used to address someone you are talking to.

★ **boludear:** 1) to mess around, to waste time, to screw off. *-Hola, ¿qué hacés? -Nada, estoy en casa **boludeando**.* 2) to bullshit someone, make up excuses to avoid something (for example, paying you). *Los inquilinos me están **boludeando** con el pago del alquiler.*

★ **boludez:** 1) trivial, not a big deal. *Te compré un regalito. Es una **boludez** pero creo que te va a gustar.* 2) something easy, simple that anyone can do. *El examen era una **boludez**, me saqué un 10. SYN:* gansada, huevada.

• **bombón** •

★ 💣 **boludo:** 1) stupid, idiot, dumbshit, may either be a serious insult or used in a playful or friendly manner. *Es un **boludo**, no se lo estaba diciendo en serio. SYN:* tarado, pelotudo, huevón, gil. 2) dude, guy, phrase to get someone's attention, generally a friend's or someone that you know. *Ché, **boludo**, decíle a Martín que traiga cerveza.*

**bomba:** a hot chick. *SYN:* bombón, camión, minón, un caño.

**bombacha:** a woman's panties. *SYN:* chabomba.

💣 **bombear:** to have sex.

**bombero:** a referee that makes bad calls against one team.

**bombilla:** the metal straw used for drinking *mate*.

**bombita:** a light bulb.

★ **bombón:** a beauty, gorgeous or hot woman. *En la fiesta estabas hecha un **bombón**, eras de lejos, la más linda.*

**Bombonera:** the soccer stadium of Boca Juniors, in the Boca neighborhood of Buenos Aires.

**bonachón:** an extremely nice person, to the point of going too far.

**boncha:** the inverse of *chabón*.

**bondi:** slang word for a bus. *Estoy viendo qué **bondi** nos deja en La Boca.*

$ **bono:** any of a number of different currencies emitted by the various provinces of Argentina as an attempt to stabilize their fiscal problems. Although the word literally means bond, they were in effect currencies printed to pay off debt.

**borrarse:** to disappear, hide, to blow someone off. *La novia le dijo que estaba embarazada y se **borró**. No **se** hizo cargo. SYN:* pirarse.

**borrego:** a kid, a teenager. *SYN:* chiquilinada

**bostero:** a term used for the Boca Juniors (soccer team) fans.

**botón:** 1) a police officer. *SYN:* rati, yuca, cana. 2) a snitch.

**botonazo:** a snitch.

**botonear:** to inform on, give someone away, betray. *Me botoneaste, sos un garga, un botonazo. SYN:* mandar al frente, buchonear.

**bragueta:** zipper. *SYN:* cierre.

★ **bronca:** anger. *Qué bronca me da que haya que esperar tanto para que te entreguen un certificado.*

**bruja:** 1) an affectionate term used with one's wife. 2) a term used for one's mother-in-law, generally not so affectionately used.

**brutal:** amazing. *El traje me quedó brutal. El sastre la tenía muy clara.*

**buchón:** a snitch, informant.

**buchonear:** to inform, give someone away, betray. *SYN:* botonear, mandar al frente.

**buitre:** a vulture, someone preying on others in a romantic way. *No te pongas esa remera ajustada que los buitres se te van a tirar encima.*

**bulín:** a bachelor's pad, an extra apartment for guys to use to score chicks.

**bulo:** a bachelor's pad.

**buraco:** a hole. *Se me hizo un buraco así de grande en los lompa.*

**burro:** racehorse. *Mi abuelo iba a los burros y se gastaba toda la jubilación en un día.*

**busarda / buzarda:** stomach or belly. *Se le nota la edad sólo por la buzarda que echó.*

**buscavida:** a person without a secure job who finds his / her way around to make ends meet doing different kinds of jobs. *Yo siempre fui un buscavidas.*

**buzón:** a large mouth.

**cabarute:** whore house.

✿ **cabecita negra:** 1) someone with black hair. 2) an extremely insulting term for a country person, much stronger than redneck or hick.

★ **caber:** to totally suit someone, to fit perfectly. *Este

# cabeza

*nuevo trabajo en Buenos Aires me re-cabe.*

**cabeza:** low class, sleazy.

**cabotaje:** a domestic flight.

**cabrón:** someone that angers easily.

**cabronearse:** to get angry, to get pissed off.

**cabulero:** superstitious. *Mi tía, cabulera, no se sentó a la mesa porque éramos 13.*

**cacerolazo:** a type of protest when the people go to the street and beat on pots (*cacerolas*) while they protest something.

**cachada:** a gag, a joke.

**cachar:** to tease, to make fun of.

**cachetada:** a face slap.

**cachetazo:** a face slap.

**cachibache:** something ridiculous.

**cachiporra:** a police night stick.

☛ **cachucha:** a woman's pussy. *SYN:* la chichi, chacón, cachufleta.

☛ **cachufleta:** a woman's pussy. *SYN:* la chichi, chacón, cachucha.

**cachuzo:** untidy, ruffled, mussed. *Me voy a dar una ducha y cambiar de ropa que estoy toda cachuza.*

**cada 2 por 3:** all the time. *Cada 2 por 3 me pregunta mi nombre. O no me registra o está gagá.*

**cada cosa:** so many of something, a lot of strange things. *Me pasa cada cosa cuando viajo.*

**cadete:** a messenger, an assistant, someone that runs errands.

**caer:** to be nabbed, get caught. *Cayó una banda narco. El cabecilla está prófugo.*

**caer bien parado:** to be successful in spite of one's bad behavior, to land on your feet.

**caer en la cuenta:** to understand something that was previously not understood. *SYN:* caerle la ficha.

**caerle la ficha:** to dawn on, to realize. *SYN:* caer en la cuenta.

**caerse de maduro:** to be obvious. *No es tan complica-*

*do, hasta te diría que **se cae de maduro**.*

**caerse(le) la baba:** when you like someone a lot. *¿No te diste cuenta que te mira y se le **cae la baba**?*

**cafiolo:** a pimp.

**cafisho / cafishio:** a pimp.

★ ☀ **cagada:** 1) an exclamation because of a mishap, Damn!, Shit! *Me saqué un 5 en el examen. **¡Qué cagada!** Necesitaba un 7 para aprobar la materia.* 2) something cheap, ugly, badly made. *Este aparato es una **cagada**, no sirve para nada.*

☀ **cagar:** 1) to screw over, to cheat. *SYN:* pifiar. 2) to shit.

☀ **cagar a golpes:** 1) to beat the heck out of someone 2) to get revenge on, to get someone back. *SYN:* cagar a palos, cagar a pedos.

★ ☀ **cagar a palos:** 1) to beat the heck out of someone. *Hubo conflictos en Plaza de Mayo y se **cagaron a palos**.* 2) to get revenge on, to get someone back. *Cuidate que te voy a **cagar a palos** si seguís bardeando.* 3) to scold. *Mi jefe me **cagó a palos** cuando le*

*dije que se había perdido el bibliorato de cuentas a pagar.*

☀ **cagar a patadas:** 1) to beat the heck out of someone. 2) to get revenge on, to get someone back. *SYN:* cagar a trompadas.

★ ☀ **cagar a pedos:** 1) to scold someone. *No me **cagues a pedos**, te dije mil veces que fue sin querer.* 2) to tell someone off.

★ ☀ **cagar a trompadas:** 1) to beat the heck out of someone. *El chorro me robó todo y encima me **cagó a trompadas**.* 2) to get revenge on, to get someone back. *Mirá, callate que te voy a **cagar a trompadas** a vos, botón. SYN:* cagar a patadas.

☀ **cagarse:** to be scared shitless. *Anoche escuché ruidos en el patio y me re **cagué**.*

☀ **cagarse de:** figuratively to die from something (laughter, cold, heat, etc.) *Me **cagué de** risa con tus amigos, salgamos otro día. / Vámonos de acá, **me estoy cagando** de frío.*

☀ **cagarse en:** to care less about, to not give a shit about.

☀ **cagarse en las patas:**

to be scared shitless.

🌑 **cagón:** a fraidy-cat, a coward.

🌑 **cajeta:** pussy. *SYN:* chichi, chacón, argolla

**calar:** to observe. *Calate a esa gorda que se le escapó una teta.*

**calavera:** a night owl, someone that functions better at night.

🌑 **calentar la pava:** to be a dick-tease. *SYN:* calienta-pijas.

🌑 **calentar la pava y no tomar el mate:** to be a dick-tease.

**calentar la silla:** literally "to warm the seat", to be at one's workstation without actually working. *Hay mucha gente al dope en la municipalidad, que van a calentar la silla.*

**calentura:** 1) sexual appetite 2) anger.

🌑 **calientapijas:** a dick-tease. *No es que le gustes, es que es una calientapijas. Calienta la pava y no toma el mate. SYN:* calentar la pava.

**caliente:** 1) horny. *Estoy caliente con la secretaria. / La secretaria me calienta.*

2) angry. *Estoy re caliente: me cobraron de más y no me aceptaron el reclamo. SYN:* al palo, en llamas.

**calor:** shame, embarrassment.

🌑 **cama redonda:** a threesome, ménage a trois.

**camelo:** a trap, a swindle, a farce.

**camión:** a sexy, attractive woman.

**camorra:** a fight, an altercation. *No busques camorra. Si dice que no, es no.*

**campana:** a lookout during a robbery.

**campera:** an informal jacket, for example a windbreaker, generally with a zipper.

**cana:** the police. *Vino la cana a mi casa anoche a llevarse a mi hermano.*

★ **canchero:** 1) cool, nice, cute. 2) nice looking. *Qué linda campera, es re canchera.*

**canillita:** a boy who delivers or sells newspapers. *En el día del canillita los puestos de diarios cierran.*

**cantar:** to confess, tell the

truth, to spill the beans.

**cantar la hora:** to tell someone what time it is. *SYN:* tirarse las agujas.

**cantar las cuarenta:** to tell someone everything that's wrong with them, getting it off your chest.

**canuto:** a stingy person.

**capanga:** a sleazy, slimy person in a position of power, as a boss.

**capo:** 1) boss. *Pregúntale al de sistemas que es un capo, la tiene clarísima en lo que es software.* 2) a fun, attractive person because of his / her personality or intelligence. *Pablito es un capo, me cae muy bien.*

💣 **cara de culo:** an angry expression.

**cara de nada:** expressionless, literally "face of nothing". *SYN:* cara de póker.

**cara de poker:** a blank, expressionless face.

**caracúlico:** a pissed off person.

**caradura:** shameless. *El caradura se anima a hacer cualquier cosa. No le tiene miedo al ridículo.*

💣 **carajo:** Shit!, Son of a bitch!

🍴 **carbonada:** a beef stew.

**carburar:** 1) to function properly. 2) to think. *SYN:* hacerse el bocho, maquinarse, darse manija.

**caretear:** to pretend or fake something that you are not, ex. pretending you have money. *Llegué a casa borracho y cuando mamá me vió, la tuve que caretear.*

**cargada:** a prank.

**cargar:** to joke about, to tease, to play a joke on. *SYN:* joder, cargosear.

**cargosear:** to tease, annoy or bother. *SYN:* joder, cargar.

**caripela:** face. *SYN:* carucha.

🍴 **carré de cerdo:** pork loin.

**cartonear:** to scavenge for cardboard.

**cartonero:** a person who scavenges for cardboard and other recyclable things in the streets of Buenos Aires in order to make a living by selling them.

# UPSIDE DOWN

*All of these words are the result of flipping
around a few letters from the original word.*

**al dope:** farting around, screwing off, not doing anything, wasting time, the inverse of *al pedo*

**boncha:** a kid or young person, the inverse of *chabón*

**chabomba:** a woman's panties, the inverse of *bombacha*

**de dorapa:** standing up, inverse of *parado*

**dolobu:** to play dumb, to pretend one has not realized what is going on, the inverse of *boludo*

**dorima:** a woman's husband, the inverse of *marido*

**el quetejedi:** the inverse of *el que te dije*, used when referring to someone you don't want others to figure out who you're talking about

**feca:** coffee, the inverse of *café*

**garca:** a swindler, a cheater, the inverse of *cagar*

**garompa:** the inverse of *poronga*

**garpar:** to pay, the inverse of *pagar*

**gomía:** friend, the inverse of *amigo*

**jermu:** a man's wife, the inverse of *mujer*

**jonca:** a casket or coffin, the inverse *cajón*

**joraca:** inversion of *carajo*

**langa:** an attractive but self-centered man, the inverse of *galán*

**los lompa:** pants

**rope:** dog, the inverse of *perro*

**telo:** The inverse of the word *hotel*, but refers more specifically when used for sexual encounters. Rooms are generally rented by the hour, for short-term occupation.

**toga:** cat, the inverse of *gato*

**tordo:** a doctor, refers to a lawyer or medical doctor, inverse of *doctor*

**trompa:** boss, owner, inverse of *patrón*

**yeca:** experience, the inverse of *calle*, literally "street" as in street smarts

**zapán:** tummy, the inverse of *panza*

**carucha:** face.

**cascar:** punish, slap or hit. *O te portás bien o te casco.*

**cascarrabia:** bad-tempered,a grump.

**casorio:** wedding.

**catinga:** a sleazy, disgusting, low-class person.

**catramina:** a vehicle on its last legs. *En esa catramina no podemos hacer 1000 kilómetros.*

**catre:** a bed.

**catrera:** a bed.

**cazar:** to understand, to capt. *No cacé el chiste, ¿vos?*

**cebar:** to serve *mate. Sé bueno, cébame un mate.*

• cerrar el pico •

**cerrar el pico:** 1) to shut up, not give away a secret or pie-ce of gossip. *Yo te cuento pero vos cerrás el pico.* 2) to cut down on food, eat less. *La única receta para estar flaca este verano es cerrar el pico.*

**chabomba:** a woman's panties, the inverse of *bombacha. SYN:* bombacha.

**chabón/a:** a kid, young person. *SYN:* pibe/a.

💣 **chacón:** cunt, pussy.

★ **chamullar:** alternate spelling of *chamuyar.*

★ **chamuyar:** to smooth talk or scam on, often in an effort to gain sexual favors. *No me chamuyés, mejor ir de frente conmigo.*

★ **chamuyero:** a smooth operator. *Es un chamuyero de aquellos. A muchas chicas, eso les gusta (Se levanta a todas las minitas, tiene mucho chamuyo).*

★ **chance:** chance, an opportunity. *Hay algún chance de que volvamos a estar juntos?*

**chanchada:** gross, disgusting. *¿Le ponés mayonesa a la ensalada? ¡Qué chanchada!*

**chancho:** 1) a pig. 2) a ticket inspector for trains and buses. *¡No! Viene el chancho y yo perdí el boleto.* 3) a boss.

**chancleta:** any type of open shoe, sandal, etc.

★ **changa:** a side job, a job to pick up some quick cash. *No tengo laburo fijo, vivo de changas.*

**chango:** a shopping cart.

**changüí:** advantage. *Si terminamos más temprano tengo 20 minutos de changüí para hacer la mía.*

★ **chanta:** fake, deadbeat, immoral, dishonest, braggart, doesn't pay debts.

**chapa:** 1) experience, résumé, background, punch your ticket to move up in a company. 2) nuts, crazy.

**chapar:** to make out, suck face. *SYN: transar, apretar, rascar.*

**chapas:** long hair.

**chapita:** nuts, crazy. *Estás medio chapita vos. SYN:* chapa.

**chasco:** 1) something you think is good and turns out to be bad. *Siempre que pido comida exótica me llevo un chasco. Es pura pinta.* 2) a dirty prank.

**chato:** 1) smashed, crushed flat. 2) a shallow (person), nothing of substance. *Es lindo, simpático, buen tipo pero muy chato. No tiene ambiciones.*

🍴 **chaucha:** string beans, green beans.

★ **ché:** this is a filler word that has no particular meaning, kind of like "Uh" or "Hey"" in English. *Ché, José, ¿por qué no venís a casa a tomar un mate hoy?*

**chicato:** to not see well, but not to the point of blindness. *¿Me leés el menú? Entre la luz baja y que soy medio chicato, no veo un pomo.*

**chiche:** 1) a toy 2) a novelty, you are delighted with for its performance or appearance. *La compu nueva es un chiche. Sólo le falta hablar.*

★ **chico/a:** kids, adolescents.

**chiflado:** crazy, nutty.

**chiflar:** to let someone know. *Si necesitás ayuda, chiflame.*

**chiflar(le) el moño:** nutty, crazy.

**chillar:** to complain.

**chimentero:** a gossip.

**chimento:** piece of gossip.

⊞ **chimichurri:** a typical Argentine sauce of olive oil, garlic and spices used for beef, generally at BBQ's.

**china:** a woman.

**chinchudo:** angry.

**chinelas:** a type of shoe or slipper with a soft base that is most often used at home, for example, slippers.

**chiquilín:** 1) a kid, a boy 2) an adult that acts like a kid.

**chiquilinada:** childish behavior, immature. *A tu edad no deberías andar con chiquilinadas.*

**chirlo:** a slap, a hit.

$ **chirola:** coins, pocket change. *Quiero renunciar al trabajo porque me pagan chirolas.*

💣 **chirusa:** an insulting term for a woman or girl. *SYN:* yiro, tilinga.

**chiva:** a goatee.

**chivar:** to sweat like a pig.

**chivarse:** to be angry, pissed off, or mad.

**chivo:** 1) an armpit 2) sweat. *¡Qué olor a chivo! SYN:* sobaco.

**chocho/a:** to be extremely happy.

**cholulo:** interested in rubbing elbows with famous people.

**chomba:** a polo shirt.

💣 **chongo:** a gay man that comes across as masculine, often to the point of hiding being gay.

**chorear:** to steal. *SYN:* afanar, currar.

⊞ **choripán:** an appetizer of sausage inside French baguette. The name comes from the combination of the Spanish words for sausage (*chorizo*) and bread (*pan*).

**chorro:** a dirty, rotten thief.

💣 **chotada:** 1) oh crap, damn, bummer. 2) something cheap, ugly, badly made. *SYN:* cagada.

💣 **choto/a:** 1) a dick. 2) something cheap, worthless. *Mi cámara vieja era re chota.*

**chucherías:** things, stuff,

generally small, inexpensive items.

**chuchi:** a girl. *SYN:* mina, tipa.

**chucho:** fear.

**chumbazo:** 1) gunshot. 2) gun. *El cana tenía un chumbazo y nos sacó corriendo.*

**chumbo:** a revolver, a weapon

• **chupamedias** •

**chupamedias:** someone who sucks up to someone else, a kiss-up or ass-kisser. *Es un chupamedias del jefe. Va a conseguir un ascenso fácilmente. SYN:* olfa.

💣 **¡Chupámela!:** I don't care what you say, screw you!

🍴 **chupar:** to drink alcohol.

🍴 **chupi:** any alcoholic drink. *SYN:* escabio.

**churro:** a hot person, nice looking.

**chusmear:** to gossip.

★ **ciento por ciento:** 100%. The more common Spanish phrase is *cien por ciento.*

**cierre:** zipper. *SYN:* bragueta.

**cimarrón:** bitter *mate.*

**cirquero:** a drama queen, someone that over-exaggerates.

**ciruja:** a street person that picks through other peoples' trash to survive. *Los cirujas son cada vez más numerosos en Buenos Aires. Se los llama cartoneros.*

**clavar:** to screw over, to cheat.

**cobanis:** police officers as referred to by thieves.

**cobrar:** to receive punishment.

💲 **cobre:** money.

**cochera:** garage.

**cocoliche:** something ridiculous.

💣 **coger:** to fuck. *SYN:* garchar, fifar, empomarse.

**cogotudo:** someone with money, an elitist.

★ 💲 **coima:** a bribe. *SYN:* un diez.

★ $ **coimear:** to bribe. *¿Yo, pagar una multa? Ni loca. Coimeo al cana y sigo de largo.*

**cojonudo:** valiant, ballsy.

**cola:** rear end.

**colarse:** to butt in, cut in a line. *No vale colarse. Cada uno espere su turno.*

**colectivo:** a bus.

**colectora:** roads that generally run parallel to highways, but do not charge the toll that the highway charges, during rush hour they are often slower since buses and trucks use these routes to avoid the tolls.

**colgarse:** 1) to be scatter-brained. *Me colgué, ¿qué me decías?* 2) to leave someone hanging  3) to mooch off of, to latch on to. *Mi hermano se colgó del cable del vecino.*

**colimba:** military service.

**colonia:** a kid's summer camp.

**comerse un garrón:** to have to bear with something unnecessarily.

💣 **comérsela:** a queer, a fag.

$ - **cometa:** a bribe.

💣 **comilón:** faggot, queer. *Ese tipo se la come.Ese tipo es un comilón.* SYN: trolo, se la come.

**como chanchos:** best friends, really close to someone.

💣 **como el culo:** bad, horrible. *SYN:* como el orto.

💣 **como el orto:** not very well, unlucky. *Me fue como el orto con mi presentación ayer. Mi jefe no me dio el aumento.* SYN: como el culo.

**como Pancho por su casa:** to enter a place as if it were one's own home, bust in as if you are the owner *Mi vecino me tiene harta. Entra como Pancho por su casa, abre la heladera, se agarra una cerveza y se pone a ver tele*

• **como sapo de otro pozo** •

**como sapo de otro pozo:** feel out of place. *Estaba mal*

# ¿cómo viene la mano?

*vestida y no conocía a nadie, me sentía **como sapo de otro pozo**.*

**¿cómo viene la mano?:** How are things working out? *A ver, **¿cómo viene la mano?** Trabajamos en equipo o individualmente?*

**compadrear:** to brag about oneself.

**compinche:** an intimate friend or family member.

★ **compu:** short for computer. *Dejé mi **compu** en casa hoy así que no te puedo dar el archivo hasta mañana.*

**con carpa:** do something subtly so people don't notice. *Entremos por esa puerta, **con carpa**, no nos van a frenar.*

**conchetear:** to behave snobbishly, being aware of fashion and latest trends. *Una banda de adolescentes **concheteando** en la puerta del boliche. / Un tipo **concheto**, que juega al rugby, vive en San Isidro y va a misa todos los domingos.*

**concheto:** snobby, stuck up. *SYN:* careta.

**concuñado/a:** an in-law by marriage, for example your sister's husband is your hus-band's *concuñado*, however he is your *cuñado*.

**conga:** a party.

• **contento como perro con dos colas** •

**contento como perro con dos colas:** extremely happy, literally "content, like a dog with two tails".

★ **copado:** cool, neat. *Está **copado** el boliche nuevo en Las Cañitas; la música y los tragos están muy buenos.* *SYN:* joya.

**copetudo:** well off, someone with money. *SYN:* cogotudo.

**corajudo:** valiant. *SYN:* cojonudo.

🐛 **cornear:** to cheat on.

**corpiño:** a bra.

## CLOTHING

**alpargatas:** kind of *gaucho* footwear made of knitted rope, canvas and an elastic opening on the upper side

**bombacha:** a woman's panties

**bragueta:** zipper

**campera:** an informal jacket, for example a windbreaker, generally with a zipper

**chabomba:** a woman's panties, the inverse of *bombacha*

**chancleta:** any type of open shoe, sandal, etc.

**chinelas:** a type of shoe or slipper with a soft base that is most often used at home, for example, slippers

**chomba:** a polo shirt

**cierre:** zipper

**corpiño:** a bra

**jardinero:** overalls, made from jeans, generally worn with a t-shirt

**lienzos:** men's underwear

**lompas:** pants

**los lompa:** pants

**malla:** a bathing suit

**mameluco:** one-piece overalls, typically used by mechanics

**mañanita:** a shawl

**pollera:** a skirt

**tamangos:** rustic shoes

**tanga:** a g-string

---

[$] **corralito:** word used to describe the step the government took in 2001 and 2002 to seize bank deposits and control the amount of money people could withdraw from their accounts.

**correr la bola:** to spread a rumor or gossip. *Se corre la bola de que Juana le mete los cuernos al novio, ¿Sabés algo?*

**correr la bolilla:** to spread gossip. *SYN:* correr la bola.

**correr la coneja / la lie-bre:** in dire straits, economically.

**cortada:** a dead end street.

★ [▯] **cortado:** an espresso coffee with a little bit of milk.

**cortina:** a lack of something.

**cotizarse:** to be worth a lot.

**cotorra:** a woman who talks nonstop, blabbermouth. *Sos una cotorra, calláte dos minutos, por favor.*

**cotorrear:** to gossip. *SYN:* chimentar, chusmear.

# country

★ **country:** a gated community, generally outside the city. *Es re concheta, vive en un* **country** *y manda a los chicos al colegio más caro de la zona.*

**cráneo:** 1) head. 2) intelligent.

**creído:** stuck up, snobby, thinks too much of him/ herself.

⊞ **crema chantilly:** whipped cream.

**crenchas:** long and messy hair.

**croqueta:** head. *SYN:* balero, bocho.

**croto:** 1) a homeless person. 2) badly or haphazardly dressed, to run out of the house for a moment.

**cruzar el charco:** to cross a river or ocean, most often in reference to crossing the Río de la Plata to Uruguay.

**cuadrado:** not smart enough to understand.

**cualquier bondi te deja bien:** 1) to be satisfied with any guy (girl) sexually. 2) indicates general ambivalence about something. *SYN:* estar regalada.

**cualquier verdura:** 1) nothing to do with, not related to in any way. 2) something without truth. *SYN:* cualquier fruta, cualquiera.

★ **cualquiera:** nothing to do with, not related to in any way. *Que decís...eso es* **cualquiera***.*

**cuando pinte:** whenever it comes up.

**cuartelazo:** military rebellion.

💣 **cuatrochi:** a nerd, four eyes.

⊞ **cucurucho:** ice cream cone.

**cucusa:** head.

**cuervo:** a lawyer.

💣 **cuete:** a fart. *La abuela está viejita y se tira* **cuetes** *camino al baño.*

**cuida (ser un cuida):** a guy that does not let his friends date his sisters or female friends.

**cuiqui:** fear, panic. *SYN:* chucho.

💣 **culear:** to fuck. *SYN:* coger, garchar, empomarse.

★ **culo:** luck. *Mi amiga reconoce que aunque trabaja mucho, a su vez tiene* **culo***.*

**cuore:** heart. *SYN:* bobo.

**curda:** drunk, messed up.

**currar:** to steal or swindle.

**curro:** 1) a thief. 2) small job. *SYN:* changa.

☞ **curtir:** to screw, not as strong as *garchar*.

☞ **curtirse:** 1) to gain experience. *Antes de trabajar de intérprete, Mercedes necesita curtirse más.* 2) to screw off. *No me importa un carajo. ¡Que se curta!*

★ **dale:** 1) yes. *¿Vamos al cine? ¡Dale!* 2) continue (speaking). *Dale, ¿y? ¿qué te dijo?* 3) go ahead. *Dale, pasá, tomá asiento.*

**dale gas:** to step on it, put the pedal to the metal. *SYN:* meterle fierro, meterle pata.

**dandy:** a Don Juan, somebody who knows how to conquer women with politeness and manners.

★ **dar bola:** to pay attention or listen to. *La mina no me dió bola cuando empecé a hablar con ella. SYN:* darle pelota.

★ **dar boliya / bolilla:** to pay attention to, to attend to. *Che, nadie me da boliya* cuan-

do digo algo. Les pedía que no alquilaran una de terror porque no me gustan.

★ **dar bronca:** to make someone mad. *Me dió bronca escuchar que habían robado a mi amigo Fabián.*

**dar cabida:** let something happen, give way for someone to do something. *Si no te gusta, no le des cabida y va a dejar de llamarte.*

**dar calce:** to give someone an opportunity or chance.

**dar la biaba:** to beat someone up.

☞ **dar masa:** to fuck, to have sex, usually used by men in reference to a sexual partner.

☞ **dar matraca:** to have sex, usually used by men in reference to a sexual partner.

**dar paja:** to feel lazy.

**dar palma:** to suddenly be tired or worn out.

**dar por las pelotas:** to be annoying.

**dar soga:** to give someone their space, cut some slack. *Si no me dan soga no puedo tomar decisiones con independencia.*

# darle a la lengua

**darle a la lengua:** to speak a lot.

**darle al diente:** to eat a lot.

★ **darle pelota:** to pay attention or listen to. *No me des pelota, estoy muy cansada y no coordino.* SYN: darle bola.

**darse manija:** to obsess with an idea, to over-think. *No te des manija con los resultados de los análisis. Sea lo que sea, no es grave.* SYN: hacerse la pelicula, hacerse el bocho, maquinarse.

**darse un palo:** to have a traffic accident. SYN: pegarse un palo.

**darse vuelta la tortilla:** to turn the tide.

**de a puchos:** a little at a time, bit by bit.

**de apoliyo:** sleeping.

**de arriba:** for free, without paying.

**de coté:** on the side, sideways.

**de cotelete:** on one side, inclined. SYN: de coté.

**de dorapa:** standing up, inverse of *parado*. *Hicimos el sexo en el avion de dorapa.*

**de garrón:** for free, without paying.

**de onda:** 1) with good intentions. 2) for free.

**de paso y cañazo:** while we're here, taking advantage of the situation. *Pasé a visitarla y de paso y cañazo, piqué algo de almuerzo.*

**de pedo:** by luck, by chance. *Casi me toca quedarme de guardia en el hospital el fin de semana pero me salvé de pedo porque le dieron la guardia a un residente nuevo.*

**dechavar / deschavar:** to snitch on, denounce.

**dejar de percha (colgado):** to stand someone up, ditch, blow off.

**del año del jopo:** extremely old.

**del año del pedo:** extremely old.

🖤 **delantera:** tits.

★ **depto:** shortened form of *departamento*, an apartment. *Alquilo un depto de dos ambientes hace 6 años ya.*

**derecho de piso:** paying or

suffering at the beginning of something, the price of admission.

**desayunarse:** to realize, become aware, get to know or learn.

**desbolado:** screwed up, messed up.

★ **desbole:** a mess, a disaster, a screw up. *Es piola pero le juega en contra que sea un desbole con los horarios y la puntualidad.*

**descartable:** disposable.

**deschavar:** to tell on, to confess, to reveal, to give away. *Nos deschavó en frente de todos. Ya nuestra relación no es un secreto.*

**deschavarse:** to become public.

💣 **desconche:** a mess, a disaster, a fuck up.

**desenchufar:** unwind, relax. *Me voy a la playa a desenchufarme un poco.*

**despachar (a alguien):** to get rid of someone.

**despacharse a gusto:** to get off your chest.

**despelotado:** totally disorganized.

**despiole:** a mess, a disaster, a screw up. *SYN:* despelote, quilombo.

**desprendido:** generous with money.

★ **día off:** a holiday. *El lunes pasado me tomé un día off para estudiar. Mañana tengo un final.*

**diario:** a newspaper.

★ **DNI:** these letters stand for *Documento Nacional de Identidad*, literally National Identity Document, the official document that everyone has for identification in Argentina. *Señor, ¿me podría mostrar su DNI o cédula? Muchas gracias.*

**dolobu:** to play dumb, to pretend one has not realized what is going on, the inverse of *bolu-do.*

**dopado:** woozy or out of it, from medicine more so than from drugs.

**dorar la píldora:** to flatter someone to get something from them, to butter them up.

**dorima:** a woman's husband, the inverse of *marido.*

# dormí

**dormí:** to miss an opportunity, to let it escape. *Cómo **dormí** con Flopi, estaba entregada y yo no hice nada.*

**dos gatos locos:** very few people.

**dulce de leche:** a caramel-like sauce widely used in Argentine cuisine. Ice cream, *alfajores*, crepes and cakes all often include *dulce de leche*.

**duranga:** hard.

**durazno:** peach, another Spanish word is *melocotón*.

**echar el ojo:** to set one's eyes on someone or something, to stare at.

**echar flit:** tell someone "to go fly a kite". *SYN:* sacar cagando.

**echarse un cago:** to shit.

**echarse un meo:** to piss.

★ **echarse un polvo:** to blow your load, to have sex (extremely vulgar, may be used for men or women). *Qué cara que tenés. ¿Hace cuánto no te **echás un buen polvo**?*

**el bombo:** a pregnant woman's womb.

**El Clásico:** This is one of the most important soccer games of the year: River (Plate) versus Boca.

★ **el cole:** short for colegio, or school. *A la salida **del cole**, vamos a la plaza a tomar mate, ¿dale?*

• **el dia que las vacas vuelen** •

**el día que las vacas vuelen:** never, when pigs fly, literally "the day that cows fly".

★ **el finde:** short for *fin de semana*, or weekend. *¿Tenés planes este **finde**?*

**el horno no está para bollos:** the situation is so delicate that it can turn worse at any moment.

**el que te dije:** a phrase referring to someone specific but without mentioning his or her name.

**el quetejedi:** the inverse of *el que te dije*, used when referring to someone you don't want others to figure out who you're talking about.

**elemento:** an annoying or bothersome person, someone low-class.

**embarrar la cancha:** to play dirty.

**embolante:** boring. *¡Qué fiesta embolante! No vinieron los más divertidos.*

**embroncarse:** to get mad, to be pissed off.

**empanada:** a small turnover, generally an appetizer or snack, with any type of filling. Common fillings are beef, corn and cheese although numerous other types of fillings are available.

**empedado:** drunk.

**empedarse:** to get drunk.

**empilcharse:** to dress up with one's best clothes.

**empilche:** elegant clothing.

**empinado:** drunk.

**empinar el codo:** to incline the elbow (as in to drink).

**empomar:** to stick it in (sexually).

**empomarse:** to have sex, used by men. *SYN:* coger, garchar, fifar, culear.

**en banda:** to be left alone.

**en bici:** on a bike. *Fuimos en bici a ver el partido de fútbol.*

• en bolas •

★ **en bolas:** 1) completely naked. *Cuando mis amigos entraron a mi depto, yo estaba en bolas, pero, por suerte, estaba muy oscuro.* 2) broke, penniless, alone, left with nothing. *Cuando vino el corralito me quedé **en bolas**.* 3) taken by surprise. *La profesora tomó un examen sorpresa y yo estaba totalmente **en bolas**.* 4) to not understand, to have no idea. *Tengo que recuperar cuatro clases. Estoy **en bolas** con matemáticas.*

**en curda:** drunk.

💣 **en la concha de la lora:** in the middle of fucking nowhere.

💣 **en la loma del culo:** in the middle of fucking nowhere.

💣 **en la loma del orto:** in the middle of fucking nowhere.

• en pampa y la vía •

**en pampa y la vía:** poor, penniless.

★ 💣 **en pedo:** 1) drunk, shit-faced, plastered. *Estaba **en pedo**, ni me acuerdo si le di un beso o no.* 2) nuts, crazy. *¿Le regalaste la computadora a tu ex? ¿Vos estás **en pedo**?*

**en solfa:** jokingly.

**en tarlipes:** naked.

**en un periquete:** right away, quickly. *SYN:* en un toque.

★ **en un toque:** to do or achieve something rapidly and easily. *No te preocupes, te lo hago **en un toque**, no cuesta nada. SYN:* en un periquete.

**en llanta:** a flat tire. *Hola, te llamo para avisarte que quedamos **en llanta** y nos retrasamos un rato.*

**enbroncarse:** to get mad, angry.

**encajado:** stuck in mud.

**encanutar:** to hoard.

**encarajinar:** to complicate.

**encarar:** to face up to.

**enchastrar:** to soil, stain or get muddy.

**enchincharse:** to get angry.

**enchufado:** literally "plugged", very interested in something.

**enconchado:** passionately in love with.

**encontronazo:** an argument, fight. *SYN: agarrada.*

**enculado:** pissed off.

💣 **encularse:** to give the silent treatment, especially from a woman.

**enfilar:** to go somewhere.

**engancharse:** to be really interested in someone, or stuck on (romantically).

**engatusar:** to cheat.

**engranarse:** to get angry, mad.

**engrupido:** thinks too much of oneself.

**engrupir:** to lie to, to trick. *Pendejo **engrupido**, entró a la empresa hace dos semanas y se hace el galán, el seductor y el jefecito.*

★ **enquilombar:** to mess up, to screw up. *Tengo toda la casa **enquilombada**.*

**ensartarse:** to get stuck doing something you don't really want to do, or when you would like to be doing something else.

**entrador:** nice.

💣 **entregar el marrón:** to get it up the ass.

**entrevero:** a mess, a screw up, a fight, a heated discussion.

**entrompado:** angry.

**es lo más:** the best.

**es una masa:** cool, fantastic.

**escabiado:** drunk.

**escabiar:** to drink to get drunk.

🍴 **escabio:** any alcoholic drink.

**escarbadientes:** toothpick.

**escrachar:** 1) to take a bad photo of someone. 2) to ruin, break.

**escrache:** a type of protest where a small group of people get together to protest another person, to call attention to something bad that another person (often a politician) did.

**escracho:** an ugly person.

**espamentoso/a:** having a big ego, full of yourself, exaggerated.

# esperar la carroza

**esperar la carroza:** 1) someone that takes a while to do something or make a decision (like getting married). 2) wait for something to happen, delay action.

**estar a pleno:** to be completely dedicated to or focused on something or someone. *SYN:* a full.

★ **estar al divino botón:** 1) to have nothing to do. *Los empleados sin tareas asignadas* **están al divino botón.** 2) to not have a use, without a function. *Mi Hi-fi tiene veinte mil funciones que* **están al divino botón.** *Nunca se usan.* *SYN:* estar al pedo.

★ **estar al pedo:** to idle about, have nothing important to do, to hang out, chill out, screwing off, wasting time, farting around. *Voy a* **estar al pedo** *hasta las 5:00, te invito a tomar un café.*

**estar al pedo como timbre de bóveda / avión:** to be worthless, to not do anything.

💣 **estar alzado:** to be horny.

**estar arruinado:** to look older than your age, tired or worn out, literally "to be ruined".

**estar careta:** for a drug user, to not be high.

**estar cebado:** literally "plugged", to be very interested in something.

**estar chupado:** to be drunk.

**estar con el bombo:** to be pregnant.

**estar con todas las pilas:** ready to go.

★ **estar copado con:** to really like, to be fascinated with. *Estoy muy copada con el libro que empecé a leer.*

**estar curtido:** to have experience. *SYN:* estar fogueado.

• **estar al pedo** •

## ALCOHOL

**birra:** a beer
**chupar:** to drink alcohol
**chupi:** any alcoholic drink
**curda:** drunk, messed up
**empedado:** drunk
**empedarse:** to get drunk
**empinado:** drunk
**en curda:** drunk
**en pedo:** drunk, shit-faced, plastered
**escabiado:** drunk
**escabiar:** to drink to get drunk
**escabio:** any alcoholic drink
**estar chupado:** to be drunk
**estar dado vuelta:** wasted, drugged, drunk
**estar del otro lado:** drunk
**fondo blanco:** bottom's up (when drinking), down the hatch
**irse p'al otro lado:** to be hammered, trashed or drunk
**mamarse:** to get drunk
**mamúa:** drunkenness
**tener un pedo bárbaro:** to be really drunk
**tintillo:** red wine
**tomado:** drunk
**tomarse un vinasi:** to have a drink of wine
**vinacho:** wine

**estar dado vuelta:** wasted, drugged, drunk.

**estar del otro lado:** drunk.

**estar de onda:** for something to be fashionable, trendy.

• **estar de pirata** •

**estar de pirata:** 1) to go out with male friends to pick up girls and cheat on your wife or girlfriend. 2) to go out with a woman in secrecy to hide that you are cheating on your wife.

# estar de rechupete

• estar de rechupete •

🍴 **estar de rechupete:** something tasty (food).

**estar duro:** to be high from cocaine.

**estar embolado:** to be bored.

**estar en cana:** to be in jail, prison.

**estar en el horno:** to be in a difficult or complicated situation.

**estar en la onda:** to be in the loop.

★ **estar en pelotas:** to not understand, to not have a clue.

**estar fogueado:** to have experience. *SYN*: estar curtido.

**estar guardado:** to be in jail.

*Mi viejo **está guardado** desde que tengo uso de razón.*

**estar hecho:** to be stuffed from eating.

**estar hecho un langa:** to be an extremely confident person, a seductor.

**estar limado:** to be burned out.

• estar meado por los gatos •

**estar meado por los gatos:** to be cursed, covered in bad luck.

**estar metido:** to be in love.

**estar pachucha:** to not feel very well, be run down, or sad.

**estar paja:** to be lazy.

**• estar para chuparse los dedos •**

🍴 **estar para chuparse los dedos:** something tasty (food).

**estar para el diván:** to be crazy. *Chiquita, estás para el diván.*

★ **estar un kilo (y dos pancitos):** excellent (even better than excellent). *El asado está un kilo (y dos pancitos). SYN:* estar bárbaro.

★ **este... ¿como es?:** so, I was saying..., this is a filler used in conversations.

**estirar la pata:** to die.

**estrolar:** to run into (as in a car accident). *Me estrolé con-*

tra un polo de luz pero la saqué barata y ni un rajuño me hice.

**expensas:** a condo fee or monthly maintenance expenses for an apartment.

★ **facha:** a person's appearance. *Que facha que tiene tu novio. Seguilo de cerca.*

★ **fachada:** face, the appearance of someone or something, usually deceitful. *Es pura fachada, no mirás para abajo porque te llevás un chasco.*

**facho:** someone on the extreme right side of politics, comes from the word for fascist.

**facón:** a type of knife common in Argentina.

🍴 **factura:** general word used to describe a group of pastries, often for breakfast (ex. medialunas, vigilantes). *Amo desayunar con facturas los domingos.*

🍴 **fainá:** a garbanzo bean based dough that is baked and then served as an appetizer.

**fajar:** to beat someone up. *SYN:* trompear.

**falluto / fayuto:** a liar.

# falopa

**falopa:** drugs.

**falopearse:** to shoot up, use drugs.

**falopero:** a drug addict.

**fanfa:** having a big ego, full of yourself, short for *fanfarrón*.

**fangote:** a lot of something. *Menem se hizo un **fangote** de guita cuando era presidente.*

**farabute:** flashy, show off.

**faroles:** eyes.

**farra:** out on the town.

**faso:** marijuana joint. It used to mean cigarette, but since smoking pot became as popular as tobacco, now it refers to pot only.

**fato:** have a sexual relationship pending, or in the works.

**feca:** coffee, the inverse of *café. Vamos a tomar un **feca** y lo charlamos, ¿te parece?*

**festejar:** to court someone, to pursue someone. *SYN:* affair.

**festichola:** a party. *Después de cenar en casa, se armó una **festichola**.*

**fetén:** excellent. *La decoración del salón estaba **fetén** fetén.*

★ **fiaca:** laziness, without energy or desire to do anything, passive, sluggish. *¡Qué **fiaca** que tengo! SYN:* laxitud, pereza, holganza.

**fiambre:** a dead body.

**fichar:** to stare at, or observe with interest. *La **fiché** toda la noche pero ella ni me miró.*

**fideo:** an extremely thin person.

**fiero:** physically ugly.

💣 **fiesta loca:** an orgy.

💣 **fiesta negra:** an orgy.

💣 **fifar:** to fuck, screw.

**firme como rulo de estatua:** 1) overeager, for example, the first person that arrives at a party. 2) pig-headed, stubborn.

**firulete:** 1) a doodle 2) in Tango, a step drawing doodles on the floor.

**flaco:** a generic term for a kid.

**flashear:** to be fascinated, to flip out excited about something.

**fletar:** to fire someone.

**flete:** a van or truck for hire.

**flotadores:** love handles.

**foguearse:** to gain experience. *SYN:* curtirse.

**fondo blanco:** bottom's up (when drinking), down the hatch.

**forrado (en guita):** rich, well off.

**forrarse (en guita):** to make a lot of money.

**forrear:** humiliate.

💣 **forro:** 1) a rubber, a condom. 2) an asshole, scumbag, shithead, jerk, idiot. *SYN:* boludo, pelotudo, gil.

**fortachón:** strong, vigorous.

**franchute:** a Frenchman.

**franela:** 1) dust rag. 2) sexual petting, rubbing or caressing.

**franelear:** to grind or rub against sexually. *SYN:* transar.

**franelero:** a cuddly person.

**frenar el carro:** to put someone in his / her place. *SYN:* parar el carro.

**fresquete:** cold.

**fruncido:** afraid.

🍴 **frutilla:** strawberry.

🍴 **fugazza:** a stuffed pizza that has no sauce or cheese, made with sweet fried onions.

🍴 **fugazzeta:** the same as *fugazza* but with mozzarella cheese.

**fulero/a:** an ugly situation or person.

**fundido:** worn out, sunk.

**fusilado:** very tired. *Me quiero sacar los zapatos y la corbata ya, estoy **fusilado**.*

**gagá:** old, mentally off, rundown.

💲 **gamba:** 1) leg. *Mirá las **gambas** que tiene esa mina.* *SYN:* pata. 2) a great pal, a true friend. *Fué el amigo más **gamba** de mi adolescencia. Me hacía la gamba en todas.* 3) one hundred pesos.

**gansada:** 1) something minor, without importance. 2) something easy. *SYN:* boludez.

**ganso:** fool, idiot, dummy. *SYN:* boludo, tarado.

**garca:** a swindler, a cheater, the inverse of *cagar.*

**garcha:** something worthless, a piece of shit. *SYN:* truchada.

# garchar

**garchar:** to fuck. *SYN:* coger, culear, fifar, empomarse.

**garfios:** fingers.

**gargajo:** a loogie. *SYN:* pollo.

**garompa:** the inverse of *poronga*.

**garpar:** to pay, the inverse of *pagar*.

**garrapiñada:** candy-coated peanuts.

**garrón:** an adverse situation. *La dejó el novio. ¡Qué garrón!*

**garronear:** to freeload, get stuff for free, bum off of, mooch off of. *SYN:* manguear.

**garúa:** a rain drizzle.

**gaseosa:** a soda, a pop.

**gasoil:** diesel.

**gasolero:** cheaply, economically, for example when going on vacation.

**gastar:** to make fun of, to mock, to tease.

**gaterío:** brothel, whore house.

**gatillar:** to spend a lot of money.

**gato:** 1) a prostitute. 2) a toupee, rug or hairpiece.

**gaucho:** the Argentine equivalent of a cowboy.

**gemelos:** cufflinks.

**gente paqueta:** refined people.

★ **gil:** fool, sucker.

**gilada:** something minor, without importance. *SYN:* boludez.

**gilún:** a fool.

**girar (decía dar un yiro):** to walk around.

**goma(s):** 1) tits. *Mirá las gomas que tiene esa mina.* 2) a goofy, dumb or foolish person. *Es gracioso el pibe pero medio goma.*

**gomía:** friend, the inverse of *amigo*.

**gorila:** politically far right.

**gozar:** to make fun of, to mock.

★ **grasa:** a lowly, slimy, disgusting person. *Está saliendo con una chica distinta a él. Habla grasa, se viste grasa...¿qué le vió?, él que es tan fino.*

**graserío:** sleazy group.

---

### PEDO

*The most versatile word in all of Argentina...*

**a los pedos:** extremely fast, in a hurry

**al pedo:** something useless, that didn't need to be done, or that was a waste of time

**cagar a pedos:** 1) to scold someone 2) to tell someone off

**de pedo:** by luck, by chance

**del año del pedo:** extremely old

**en pedo:** 1) drunk, shitfaced, plastered 2) nuts, crazy

**estar al pedo:** to idle about, have nothing important to do, to hang out, chill out, screwing off, wasting time, farting around

**estar al pedo como timbre de bóveda/avión:** to be worthless, to not do anything

**ni en pedo:** No way! Out of the question! Forget it!

**salir en un pedo:** to head out quickly

**tener un pedo bárbaro:** to be really drunk

---

**grasún:** something of bad taste, out of place. *SYN:* grasa, mersa, groncho, cabeza.

**gratarola:** free, without cost.

**grela:** scum, dirt. *Qué grela que hay en esta pocilga.*

**gronchada:** sleazy. *SYN:* grasada, mersada.

**groncho:** sleazy, disgusting, low class. *SYN:* grasoso.

★ ✹ **guacho:** slime ball, jerk, but often used in a playful sense among friends.

**guapo:** macho, headstrong.

*No te hagas el guapo conmigo que te llevo dos cabezas.*

★ **guarangada:** something vulgar.

**guarango:** someone acting vulgar.

**¡guarda!:** Look out! Pay attention! Be careful!

**guardado:** imprisoned.

**guardilla:** attic.

⊞ **guarnición:** a side dish, the more common Spanish term is *acompañamiento.*

★ **guasada:** 1) something

# guaso

gross, vulgar. *Contó cada* **guasada** *que quedamos asqueados.* 2) excessive, in excess. *¡Epa! Me serviste una* **guasada**. *No puedo comer tanto.*

★ **guaso:** gross, disgusting, ill-mannered.

★ $ **guita:** bucks, money. *Ché, ¿tenés* **guita** *para una birra?*

**guitarrear:** to completely improvise something, to bullshit, to make up.

**gurí:** a boy.

**gurisa:** a girl.

**gurrumín:** a kid. *SYN:* pibe.

**hacer bardo:** to mess up, to screw up, to make things worse.

**hacer boleta:** to kill.

★ **hacer bolsa a alguien:** to beat the hell out of someone, to destroy someone. *Estábamos bailando y me pisó. Me* **hizo bolsa** *los dedos del pie.*

**hacer borregadas:** to screw around, to do stupid stuff.

★ **hacer cagadas:** to screw up or mess up. *Me estás mirando mal. ¿Hice alguna cagada?*

💣 **hacer el siete:** to have anal sex.

**hacer el verso:** to smooth talk or cheat someone, sell them a bill of goods.

**hacer footing:** to jog.

**hacer gancho:** to fix you up with someone, make a connection with, for example a guy asks his friend to ask a girl if she likes him.

**hacer giratoria la puerta:** said when a door is slammed hard.

• hacer huevo •

**hacer huevo:** to not do anything, screw off. *Hice huevo todo el fin de semana.*

**hacer la gamba:** to lend a

hand, to help out.

**hacer la pata:** to lend a hand, to help out.

**hacer la tuya, la mía:** to do what you feel like doing without any interference. *Nos juntamos a cenar temprano y después cada uno hace la suya.*

**hacer la vista gorda:** to overlook.

**hacer noni:** to sleep, go to bed. *Me voy a hacer noni ya. Mañana madrugo.*

**hacer pucherito, pucheros:** the expression on one's face before actually crying, scrunching up your face, often used by women to get what they want from a guy.

💣 **hacer un pete:** to give a blowjob.

**hacer una vaquita:** to chip in.

**hacerse el bocho:** to fantasize about something.

★ **hacerse el boludo:** to play dumb, to pretend one has not realized what is going on.

**hacerse el canchero:** to compliment oneself, to brag often to the point of sounding ridiculous.

**hacerse el guapo:** to come across as macho, better than others.

**hacerse el otario:** to pretend like you don't understand, to play the fool.

**hacerse el piola:** to try to act smart, to be sly, cunning.

**hacerse el sota:** to remain quiet while observing or listening to others.

**hacerse humo:** to escape.

**hacerse la paja:** to jerk off.

★ **hacerse la pelicula:** to obsess with an idea, to overthink. *Con el dolor de estómago que tenía me hice la pelicula de que era cáncer. SYN:* darse manija.

**hacerse la rata:** to skip school. *SYN: ratearse.*

**hasta las bolas:** very busy or involved in something.

**hasta las manos:** very busy or involved in something.

**hecho percha:** destroyed.

★ **hincha:** a fan (sports, etc.). *Soy hincha de Boca hasta la muerte.*

**hinchabolas:** pain in the ass,

# hinchacocos

annoying, literally "swell the balls". *¡No me rompas las pelotas!. ¡Sos un **hinchabolas**!*

**hinchacocos:** bothersome, annoying.

**hinchaguindas:** annoying, bothersome, unbearable.

★ **hinchapelotas:** pain in the ass, annoying. *El **hinchapelotas** de mi hermano me llama hasta para preguntarme cómo se apaga la luz.*

★ **hinchar:** to annoy, to bother.

★ **hincharse las pelotas:** to bother, to bug, to annoy. *No me **hinches las pelotas**, te voy a depositar el dinero que te debo hoy, como te prometí.*

★ **hoy por hoy:** nowadays. *Hoy por hoy las cosas no están bien en la economía.*

**huevada:** something unimportant or insignificant.

**huevos:** balls, nuts.

🍴 **humita:** a corn filling used in *empanadas*.

★ **imbancable:** annoying, someone that you cannot stand or put up with. *Esa mina es **imbancable**. Llega y se pone a dar órdenes.*

• inútil como cenicero de moto•

**importar un corno:** to not care about something.

**importar(le) (a uno) un carajo:** to not give a damn. *Me importa un carajo si Juan quiere salir con mi hermana.*

**indio/a:** a screw-up.

**inflar:** to bug, bother or annoy.

• intútil como bocina en avión •

**inútil como bocina en avión:** someone or something useless, literally "useless like a plane's horn"

**Inútil como cenicero de moto:** someone or something useless, literally "useless like a motorcycle's ashtray".

**ir a los papeles:** 1) to cut to the chase, to get down to business. 2) to go straight to sex.

• ir a los yuyos •

**ir a los yuyos:** to sneak off and have sex (ex. in the bushes). *Ese chavón esta para **irse a los yuyos**. SYN:* andar en los yuyos.

★ **ir como piña:** to fit in well. *Agrégale albahaca, **va como piña** con el tomate.*

**ir / estar de farra:** to live it up.

**irse al bombo:** 1) to die. 2) to fail financially, go bankrupt.

**irse al carajo:** to go too far, exaggerate. *Compró 3 docenas de facturas, **se fue al**

*carajo*. / *Me dijo imbécil, **se fue al carajo**.*

**irse de mambo:** to go nuts, to go crazy, to go off on someone, to go too far.

**irse de rosca:** to go too far.

**irse p'al otro lado:** 1) to be hammered, trashed or drunk. 2) to die.

**jabón:** fear.

**jamones:** large legs or thighs, for a woman.

**jardinero:** overalls, made from jeans, generally worn with a t-shirt.

**jermu:** a man's wife, the inverse of *mujer*.

• jeta •

**jeta:** face.

# jetón

**jetón:** a large-mouthed person or someone with a large face.

★ **joda:** 1) a prank, joke. *No te lo tomés así, era una joda.* 2) a party, a lively gathering. *Nos fuimos de joda a la costa con los pibes.*

**joder:** to tease or make fun of, to joke with.

🛥 **jodido:** messed up, fucked up, screwed up.

**jodón:** somebody annoying, bothersome, gets on your nerves.

**jonca:** a casket or coffin, the inverse of *cajón.*

**joraca:** inversion of *carajo. No veo un joraca. Prendé la luz.*

**jovato:** old, an old person.

**joya:** great, cool, sounds like fun, okay.

**joya nunca taxi:** well kept, in great condition, as good as new.

**joya:** great, cool.

**jugado:** bold, daring, to have balls to do something.

**jugársela:** to dare to do something, to bet the farm.

*SYN:* mandarse.

**julepe:** a scare.

**julepeado:** scared.

**juntarla con pala:** to earn a lot of money, especially lately.

**justiniano:** just the right amount, limited.

**kaput:** 1) when something breaks down. 2) when someone dies. *¿Te acordás de la abuela de Marcos? Bueno, kaput.*

★ **know how:** in-depth knowledge of something, experience. *El know how que tiene ese ingeniero sobre diseños de empaques es único en la industria.*

**la clásica:** something typical.

🛥 **la concha de la lora:** 1) mother-fucker, son of a bitch, especially used when you injure yourself, or something breaks or is stained. 2) Timbuktu, really far away.

🛥 **la concha de tu madre:** an extremely strong insult to someone, similar to mother-fucker.

**la Conchinchina:** in the middle of nowhere, far away.

**la crema:** la crème de la crème, high class, the elite.

★ **la facu:** short for *la facultad*, another term for college or university. *Fui a **la facu** hoy para registrarme en las nuevas clases.*

**la guadaña:** death.

💣 **la mira con cariño:** a queer, a fag. *Hice que saliera con chicas, pero me da la impresión de que **la mira con cariño**.*

💣 **la re-puta que te parió:** an extremely strong insult to someone, literally "the extreme slut that gave birth to you".

**laburador:** hard-working.

**laburante:** hard-working.

★ **laburar:** to work. *Estuve **laburando** todo el día. No me dio tiempo ni siquiera para almorzar.*

★ **laburo:** work, a job. *Estoy buscando cualquier tipo de **laburo**; hace tres meses que estoy en la calle.*

**lágrima:** hot milk served with just a little bit of coffee.

★ **lance:** a shot, to take a shot.

**lancero:** a man that throws himself at women.

**langa:** an attractive but self-centered man, the inverse of *galán*.

**lapicera:** fountain pen.

**largavistas:** literally "long views", binoculars.

**largo:** tall.

**las chicas:** a female group of friends.

🍴 **lastrada:** food.

🍴 **lastrar:** to eat.

**le falta un jugador:** to be crazy, nutty, literally "he / she has a player missing".

💣 **leche de mipalo:** cum.

**lenteja:** a slow person. *Esa **lenteja** que tienen trabajando en el kiosko no puede contar a diez.*

★ **levantar:** to conquer (a woman). *El sábado me **levanté** a una morocha hermosa.*

**levantar en peso:** to scold.

**levante:** a love conquest.

🍴 **licuado:** a fruit shake, made with water or milk.

# lienzos

**lienzos:** men's underwear.

**lime:** craziness.

**linyera:** a hobo, a homeless person.

**listo el pollo, pelada la gallina:** we're all set, we're ready.

**llevar el apunte:** to pay attention. *No le **lleves el apunte**, te lo dice para molestarte.*

**llevarse puesto:** to run into or bump into something.

**lo la:** short for *lo lamento*, sorry, too bad.

**lo más campante:** relaxed, without inhibitions, feeling comfortable with a situation. *Entró **lo más campante**, como si no hubiese hecho nada.*

**lo más pancho:** relaxed, chilled out, carefree.

**lo/la tengo ahí:** he/she is head over heels for me, completely in love with me.

**locólogo:** a shrink.

★ **locutorio:** a phone booth generally within a business that allows you to make a call and pay for it when you hang up, change is not required. *Me cortaron el teléfono, te llamo desde el **locutorio**. Tengo uno a la vuelta de casa.*

**lolas:** boobs.

**lompas:** pants.

**loro:** a person who talks non-stop, literally "parrot".

**los lompa:** pants. *Se me hizo un buraco así de grande en los lompa.*

**los pibes:** a male group of friends.

★ Ⓢ **luca:** one thousand of a currency, one luca is a thousand dollars or pesos.

Ⓢ **luca verde:** a thousand US dollars.

**lunfa:** short for *lunfardo*.

**lunfardo:** the name for the slang / language that has developed from the tango style of singing and dance.

**¡Ma sí!:** I don't care! *¡Ma sí! Le mando el informe como está y que se arregle sola.*

**macana:** 1) a lie, something ridiculous or off the wall. 2) a mistake.

**macanear:** to lie.

★ **macanudo:** used to describe someone fun to hang

# mandar fruta

out with. *Jorge es macanudo, me cayó bien. Invitálo a la fiesta.*

**machete:** a cheat sheet.

★ **mala leche:** 1) bad luck. *Era solamente mala leche que me robaron la billetera.* 2) bad intention.

**malandra:** a delinquent, bad person.

**malandrín:** a delinquent.

**malevo:** someone looking for a fight. *Con esa actitud de malevo se gana el rechazo de la mayoría.*

★ **malla:** a bathing suit. *¿Trajiste tu malla para tomar sol durante el viaje?*

**mamarse:** to get drunk.

**mambo:** a confusion or problem, but that is often a conflict one makes up and exaggerates in one's mind. *SYN:* quilombo.

**mameluco:** one-piece overalls, typically used by mechanics.

**mamerto:** clumsy.

**mamúa:** drunkenness.

**mañanita:** a shawl.

**mandamás:** boss, superior.

**mandar a alguien al carajo:** tell somebody to go to hell. *Le mandé al carajo cuando me dijo que se acostó con otra chica.*

**mandar al frente:** to inform on, give someone away, betray. *SYN:* buchonear, botonear

★ **mandar cualquiera:** to do something without thinking, that doesn't make sense, without knowing if it is true, and even more so when it is proven to be incorrect or false. *Me mandé cualquiera hoy en el examen; no contesté nada bien.*

• mandar fruta •

**mandar fruta:** 1) to say something not true. *No estu-*

# mandarse

*dié para el examen,* **mandé fruta**, *cualquier verdura. SYN:* mandar cualquiera. 2) not related to in any way.

**mandarse:** to step out on a limb, to do something or go somewhere without being sure one will succeed. *A las 2 de la mañana* **me mandé** *a ver mi ex-novio para pedir perdón.*

**mandarse un moco:** to make a mistake. *¡No se cómo mierda vamos a arreglar este* **moco que te mandaste!!**

☝ **manducar:** to eat.

**manganeta:** a trap, swindle.

**mangazo:** the process of asking for something way beyond reasonable, out of place, often in reference to money.

★ $ **mango:** 1) money. 2) very little or none (in reference to money). *Préstame* **cinco mangos** *para comprar una coca.*

**manguear:** to ask for something, but beyond being reasonable, to mooch off of. *SYN:* garronear.

**manguero:** someone that is always bumming stuff from other people, a freeloader.

**manija:** influence, power.

**manyate esta:** listen to what I gotta tell you, listen up.

**máquina:** 1) over-energetic. 2) a very good car or device that works fast.

**maquinarse:** to blow up a scenario in one's head. *Me* **maquiné** *con que mi marido me ponía los cuernos y le hice un escándalo al pobre santo. SYN:* darse manija, hacerse el bocho.

💣 **maraca:** a queer.

**marimacho:** a woman who looks or behaves like a man.

**mariposón:** effeminate, gay.

**marmota:** clumsy, dumb.

**marote:** a head. *Estás mal del* **marote** *vos.*

**más asustado que perro en bote:** really scared, literally "more scared than a dog in a boat".

**más perdido que Adán en el día de la madre:** be completely lost, literally "more lost than Adam on Mother's Day".

**más solo que Kung Fu:** all alone.

**masa:** 1) an attractive, interesting person. 2) something of high quality.

**masoca:** sentimental, for example after a breakup, a masochist. *Re-masoca la mina, escucha toda la música que le hace acordar a su ex-novio.*

**masoquearse:** to make yourself suffer. *Mé masoqueé escuchando a Mariah Carey, quien siempre me hace pensar en mi ex.*

🍴 **matambre:** 1) a dead body. 2) layer of meat cut from between the skin and the rib cage of cows and pigs typical to Argentine barbeques. 3) a type of dish made by spreading ingredients (ex. carrots, eggs) on top of a flat piece of meat, rolling up the meat and then cutting it in slices.

🍴 **mate:** 1) a bitter tea that is almost a religious experience for many Argentines, the process of drinking mate is often more social than anything else  2) the special container from which the tea is drunk.

**matete:** a mess, a hodgepodge. *Me hice un mate-te con el papelerío que*

no encuentro los datos que estoy buscando. SYN: quilombo.

**matina:** in the morning.

**matonear:** to intimidate.

**matufia:** something shady, mafia-style.

**me cacho en 10:** a more polite way of saying *me cago en 10.*

💣 **me cago en 10:** Shit! Son of a bitch!, a phrase used when something bad happens.

**me cayó un muerto:** to receive an unexpected job.

💣 **me chupa un huevo:** I don't give a shit.

**me comí la vida, me dormí la vida:** to do something in excess.

★ **me gusta mal:** to really like something. *Viste la nueva pelicula de Almodóvar? Sí, me gusta mal, ya la vi dos veces.*

**me importa una garompa:** to not care about something.

**me las piro:** I'm going.

**me mandé para allá:** to head for, go towards, especially when going implies risk

# me saca

of any kind.

**me saca:** it drives me nuts, it puts me in a bad mood, makes me mad.

## • mear fuera del tarro •

**mear fuera del tarro:** to be wrong, to make a mistake, literally "to piss outside the pot". *Estás **meando fuera del tarro** porque no sabés cómo fueron las cosas.*

**media naranja:** your better half, your perfect match.

🍴 **medialuna:** a small croissant most often served for breakfast. When you order a *medialuna* the follow-up question from the waiter will always be *Manteca o Grasa*? *Manteca* is a butter-based croissant that is sweet. The *Grasa* version is lard-based and not as sweet as the croissant from *manteca*.

**melenudo:** to have a lot of hair.

💣 **melones:** boobs, tits. *Che, viste los **melones** que tiene esa mina?*

**meloso:** extremely romantic. *Ya más que romántico, yo diría que es un **meloso**.*

**menesunda:** 1) an embarrassing or complicated situation, a sticky situation. 2) a mess, a disaster.

**meódromo:** a toilet.

**merca:** cocaine.

**merengue:** a difficult, complicated or messed up situation.

**mersa:** a low class, slimy, sleazy, disgusting person. *SYN:* grasa, grasoso.

**mersada:** something cheap, of low quality.

**mersún:** something cheap, of low quality.

**metejón:** infatuation, to have a crush on someone. *Hasta que no se me vaya el **metejón** que tengo con mi jefe, no me voy a concentrar en mi trabajo.*

**meter el perro:** to cheat

someone.

**meter un gancho:** to punch someone.

**meterle fierro:** to step on it, to put the pedal to the metal, to get going. *SYN:* meterle pata, dale gas.

**meterle pata:** to step on it, put the pedal to the metal. *SYN:* meterle fierro, darle gas.

**metiche:** a meddlesome person.

**micro:** a bus that travels long distances.

★ **microcentro:** the downtown part of the city of Buenos Aires. *Nuestras oficinas se encuentran en pleno **microcentro** porteño.*

🍴 **milanesa:** a breaded, fried piece of flattened beef or chicken.

🍴 **milanesa napolitana:** a *milanesa* (beef or chicken) with tomato sauce and mozzarella cheese on top.

🍴 **milanga:** see *milanesa*.

**milonga:** a dance party where Tango is played and danced to.

★ **mina, minita:** a babe, a bombshell, a chick.

**minga:** Never!

**minón:** a hot woman.

**minusa:** a hot woman.

★ **mirá vos:** What do you know?, How about that?, Go figure, Would you look at that? *¿Sabías que Pamela sale con Carlitos? ¿Si? **Mirá vos**, no tenia idea.*

**mis efectos:** close friends and family.

**mishiadura:** poverty.

**mitá y mitá:** fifty-fifty.

**miti y miti:** fifty-fifty.

**mocoso/a:** a kid, literally "snot-nosed".

**mogólico:** a fool.

**mondadientes:** a toothpick.

**moneda corriente:** very common.

**mongo aurelio:** Joe Blow.

**montoto:** Joe Blow.

🍴 **morfar:** to eat.

**morfarsela:** to be queer, gay, a fag.

🍴 **morfi:** food.

# morlaco

$ **morlaco:** money.

**morondanga:** cheap, poor quality.

🍴 **morrón:** bell pepper, other Spanish words include *pimiento* and *pimentón* depending on the country.

**mortadela:** a dead person. *SYN:* fiambre, matambre.

$ **mosca:** money.

**mosquita muerta:** a woman that comes across as inoffensive, but really is clever and / or dangerous.

**mosquitero:** a window screen.

**mostrar la hilacha:** to show a negative, weak aspect that one has managed to hide.

**mufa:** a jinx. *SYN:* yeta.

**mula:** to cheat in an inoffensive manner, like when children play.

**mulero:** a cheater. *Ganó por mulero, hizo mula, no vale.*

**mutis:** silent, quiet.

**mutis por el foro:** to sneak out quietly from something.

**muzarela:** silence.

**nabo/a:** 1) penis. 2) a fool, a nerd, a slow person, clueless, not very bright. *Te manchaste la camisa con helado,* **nabo**. *SYN:* ganso, boludo, tarado.

**nada:** a sentence filler, similar to "like" in English.

**nafta:** gasoline.

**napia:** nose.

**naso:** nose.

**nene, nena:** 1) literally a kid but often an insulting term meaning implicitly that the person is immature. 2) used to refer to a young person one is talking to.

**ni a ganchos:** No way! Out of the question! Forget it!

**ni a palos:** No way! Out of the question! Forget it!

**ni a patadas en el orto:** literally "not even with kicks in the ass", No way! Out of the question! Forget it!

**ni ahí:** No way! Not even close!

★ **ni bola:** not pay attention to, to ignore. *No vale la pena reclamar porque en la oficina de Servicio al Consumidor no te dan* **ni bola**. *SYN:* ni pelota.

★ 💣 **ni en pedo:** No way! Out of the question! Forget it!

**ni mamada:** Don't even think about it!

**ni pelota:** not pay attention to, to ignore. *SYN:* ni bola.

**ni pincha ni corta:** he / she doesn't have a say. *El director ni pincha ni corta, las decisiones las toma la gerenta.*

**ni por las tapas:** No way! Not even close!

**no entender un carajo:** to not understand a damn thing.

**no entender un cazzo:** to not understand a bit.

**no entender un pomo:** to not understand a bit.

**no hacerle ni sombra:** to not even be close in comparison. *Como jugador de fútbol Beckham no le hace ni sombra a Pelé. SYN:* no llegarle ni a los talones.

**no hay historia:** No problem!

**no llegarle ni a los talones:** to not even be close in comparison. *SYN:* no hacerle ni sombra.

★ **no pasa nada:** no big deal. *No pasa nada, queda-*

*te tranquilo, anulamos la factura y listo.*

**no pasa naranja:** nothing happening, nothing going on, no spark between two people.

**no querer más lola:** to be tired of something, to want something to end.

**no tener un cobre:** to be broke, to not have any money. *No me voy de vacaciones, no tengo un cobre.*

★ **no tener un mango:** to be broke, to not have any money.

**no tener vuelo:** to be mediocre, to not have grand plans in life.

★ **no valer un mango:** to be worth-less (a person or an object). *Por eso no vale un mango / no vale ni dos mangos.*

**nudo:** a traffic jam.

**ñata:** nose.

**ojete:** luck.

**ojo:** 1) be careful, look out. *Ojo, mi tío dice que es una truchada.* 2) hold on a minute, not so fast. *Ojo, a veces cenamos antes.*

**ojo al piojo:** Pay attention!

# olfa

Be careful! *Ojo al piojo*, me *extraña araña*.

**olfa:** a kiss up, a suck up.

**olor a chivo:** armpit odor.

**ómnibus:** a bus.

**opa:** an idiot

**oreja:** a kiss up, a suck up.

**ortiba:** with bad vibes.

★ **orto:** an ass, most often in reference to the body part. *Este jean te hace re buen orto.*

**otario:** a fool.

**paco:** a cheap form of smokeable cocaine.

⑪ **pájaro que comió voló:** to eat and run.

**pajarón:** stupid.

**pajuerano:** 1) a country bumpkin. 2) a foreigner.

**pala:** cocaine.

**pálida:** bad news.

**palmar:** 1) to be tired out. *La excursión en kayak me palmó / me dejó palmada.* 2) to pass away. *La vieja del 5to palmó hace ya unos años.* 3) to stop working. *Palmó mi cámara de fotos en la mitad del viaje.*

★ Ⓢ **palo:** a million.

Ⓢ **palo verde:** a million dollars. *Los diputados con mansiones de un palo verde son moneda corriente en este país.*

**palo y a la bolsa:** an easy woman, a slut.

⑪ **palta:** avocado, another Spanish word is *aguacate*.

⑪ **pan negro:** wheat bread.

⑪ **pan pebete:** a kind of bread similar to the one used for hotdogs and hamburgers, often used for making sandwiches.

⑪ **pancho:** a hot dog.

**papa frita:** stupid.

**paparulo:** stupid.

⑪ **papas noisette:** small, round potatoes that are baked or fried.

**papelón:** 1) an embarrassing situation. 2) a bluff. *SYN:* blef.

**papusa:** extremely beautiful (for women), a knockout.

★ **pará:** Wait a minute! Hold

on! *¡Pará! Ya discutimos esto dos veces. No es necesario repetirlo.*

💣 **paraguas:** insulting term for Paraguayans.

**parar el carro:** put someone in his / her place. *SYN:* frenar el carro.

**pasar calor:** to be embarrassed.

**pasarse de vivo:** to believe you're smarter than others without really being so.

**pasta:** cocaine.

**patente:** 1) a vehicle's license plate. 2) clearly.

**patota:** a gang.

**patovicas:** a bouncer.

**patrón:** boss-man.

★ **pavada:** 1) small, immaterial or insignificant, a trinket. *El regalo de navidad que nos dieron en la empresa fue una* **pavada**. 2) ridiculous, senseless. *¡Dejá de decir* **pavadas**! 3) easy, a piece of cake, not a big deal. *El examen fue una* **pavada**, *lo terminé en 15 minutos.*

**pavo:** 1) a fool. 2) rear-end, heinie. *¡Que* **pavo** *que tiene*

*esa mujer!*

**payasada:** 1) something small or insignificant. 2) ridiculously funny.

**pebete (pebeta):** a kid.

★ **pedante:** pompous, arrogant. *Se cree mil, es muy* **pedante**.

**pegar el raje:** to fire someone.

**pegar un baile:** to win by a lot, a beating, a drumming. *Boca le* **pegó un baile** *a River y ganaron 6 a 2.*

**pegar un bife:** to slap someone.

**pegarse un palo:** to have a traffic accident. *El cadete* **se pegó un palo** *con la moto por la lluvia. SYN:* darse un palo.

**pelmazo:** nerd.

**pelotudez:** something stupid.

★ **pelotudo:** idiot, jerk.

**pendejada:** an immature act.

**pendex:** someone young or younger than everyone else around.

**percanta:** a woman, especially in reference to a partner, girlfriend or spouse.

# perdido como turco en la neblina

**perdido como turco en la neblina:** completely lost.

**performance:** an object's ability to work properly, it's performance.

**peringundines:** 1) a dance hall. 2) a brothel, whorehouse.

**petacón:** short, stocky man.

☞ **pete:** a blowjob

**petizo:** a short, stocky person.

**piantao:** crazy, wacko, nuts.

**piantarse:** to leave quickly, scram, split.

★ **pibe/a:** 1) a kid. *Juan es un pibe, no llega a los 20.* 2) dude, man. *Acaban de asaltar al pibe que atiende la verdulería.*

**pichicata:** an injection of something.

**pichicho:** a small dog.

**pifiar:** to screw up, miss the target, goof, mess up.

☞ **pija:** dick.

**pijotero:** cheap, stingy.

★ **pilas:** 1) batteries. 2) energy, motivation. *Ponéte las pilas; tenemos que salir ya!*

**pilcha:** the best clothes you own.

**pileta:** a pool, the more common Spanish word is *piscina*. *Si quieres vamos a la quinta mañana y nos quedamos en la pileta todo el día.*

**pillado:** stuck up. *Demasiado pillado de sí mismo, se cree mil.*

**pingo:** a horse.

**pinta:** appearance. *SYN:* facha.

**pintón:** attractive, handsome.

★ **piola:** 1) with it, on the ball, clever, astute. 2) nice, friendly. 3) cool, good, excellent. 4) calm, relaxed, stay in control.

**pipi cucu:** something perfect.

**piquetero:** a picketer, someone that pickets or protests.

**pirado:** to be crazy. *Quedó medio pirada después de la muerte de su marido.*

**pirao:** crazy, nuts.

**pirarse de un lugar:** to leave quickly, scram, split.

**pispear:** to perceive something.

**pitada:** a puff of a cigarette.

## FOOD

**aceto:** balsamic vinegar, a more common Spanish word is *vinagre balsámico*

**alcaucil:** artichoke, the more common Spanish word is *alcachofa*

**alfajor:** a cookie-like sweet often made with *dulce de leche* and covered in chocolate, although a variety of types and flavors exist

**ananá:** pineapple, the common Spanish word is piña

**bife a caballo:** beef with fried eggs and French fries

**bizcocho:** oval crackers that accompany *mate*

**carbonada:** a beef stew

**carré de cerdo:** pork loin

**chaucha:** string beans, green beans

**chimichurri:** a typical Argentine sauce of olive oil, garlic and spices used for beef, generally at BBQ's

**choripán:** an appetizer of sausage inside French baguette. The name comes from the combination of the Spanish words for sausage (*chorizo*) and bread (*pan*).

**cortado:** an espresso coffee with a little bit of milk

**crema Chantilly:** whipped cream

**cucurucho:** ice cream cone

**dulce de leche:** a caramel like sauce widely used in Argentine cuisine. Ice cream, alfajores, crepes and cakes all often include *dulce de leche*

**durazno:** peach, another Spanish word is *melocotón*

**empanada:** a small turnover, generally an appetizer or snack, with any type of filling. Common fillings are beef, corn and cheese although numerous other types of filling are available

**estar de rechupete:** something tasty (food).

**estar para chuparse los dedos:** something tasty (food).

**factura:** general word used to describe a group of pastries, often for breakfast (ex. *medialunas, vigilantes*)

**fainá:** a garbanzo bean based dough that is baked and then served as an appetizer

**frutilla:** strawberry

**fugazza:** a stuffed pizza that has no sauce or cheese, made with sweet fried onions

## FOOD, *continued*

**fugazzeta:** the same as *fugazza* but with mozzarella cheese

**garrapiñada:** candy-coated peanuts

**guarnición:** a side dish, the more common Spanish term is *acompañamiento*

**humita:** a corn filling used in *empanadas*

**lastrada:** food

**lastrar:** to eat

**manducar:** to eat

**matambre:** layer of meat cut from between the skin and the rib cage of cows and pigs typical to Argentine barbeques 2) a type of dish made by spreading ingredients (ex. carrots, eggs) on top of a flat piece of meat, rolling up the meat and then cutting it in slices

**medialuna:** a small croissant most often served for breakfast. When you order a *medialuna* the follow-up question from the waiter will always be *Manteca o Grasa?* *Manteca* is a butter-based croissant that is sweet. The *grasa* version is lard-based and not as sweet as the croissant from *manteca*.

**milanesa:** a breaded, fried piece of flattened beef or chicken

**milanesa napolitana:** a *milanesa* (beef or chicken) with tomato sauce and mozzarella cheese on top

**milanga:** see *milanesa*

**morfar:** to eat

**morfi:** food

**morrón:** bell pepper, other Spanish words include *pimiento* and *pimentón* depending on the country

**pájaro que comió voló:** to eat and run

**palta:** avocado, another Spanish word is *aguacate*

**pan negro:** wheat bread

**pan pebete:** a kind of bread similar to the one used for hotdogs and hamburgers, often used for making sandwiches

**pancho:** a hot dog

**papas noisette:** small, round potatoes that are baked or fried

**pochoclo:** popcorn

**pomodoro:** tomato sauce

**pororó:** popcorn

---

### FOOD, *continued*

**postre vigilante:** a dessert of pieces of cheese and quince paste

**provoleta:** a melted cheese appetizer with spices and sometimes sausage or bell peppers on top, often grilled

**puchero:** a casserole

**raba:** calamari, the more common Spanish word is also *calamari*

**remolacha:** beet, another Spanish word is *betarraga*

**salsa criolla:** a sauce of chopped red bell pepper, onion and vinegar used to put on top of beef

**salsa rosada:** a pasta sauce that is a mix of tomato sauce and alfredo sauce, thus the name *salsa rosada* ("pink sauce" in Spanish)

**scarparo:** pasta sauce with tomato, olive oil, garlic, basil, and cream

**sorrentino:** a large ravioli-like type of pasta

**suprema napolitana:** a *milanesa* with melted cheese and tomato sauce on top

**tarta:** quiche

**tostado mixto:** a toasted ham and cheese sandwich on bread

**tuco:** tomato sauce

---

**pituco:** elegant, aristocratic.

**pitulín:** penis.

**pituto:** a thingy.

**placár:** closet.

★ **planta baja:** The street-level entry floor of a building. The second floor is almost always numbered 1, so for example an office on the 5th floor (according to the elevator and address) would actually be on the 6th story of a building. *Se vende hermoso departamento en **planta baja**, con patio de 2x1.5 al fondo.*

🍽 **pochoclo:** popcorn.

**polenta:** strength.

**pollera:** a skirt.

# pollo

**pollo:** a loogie.

🍴 **pomodoro:** tomato sauce.

**ponéle la firma:** I'm positive, 100% sure it's gonna happen.

**poner el gancho:** to sign a document.

**poner en vereda:** to draw the line in the sand, to put a limit to something.

**ponerle fichas:** to put one's support behind something thinking it will happen, for example a relationship or a business venture.

**ponerse:** 1) get down to work. *Historia es una materia fácil pero hay que ponerse.* 2) spend a large amount of money. *Para mi primer aniversario con mi novio me puse, le compré una guitarra.*

**ponerse la gorra:** to pretend your the boss, take charge.

★ **ponerse las pilas:** to get to work, get moving. *Ponéte la pilas así terminás antes de las 8 y venís al cine conmigo.*

**ponerse las Varta:** to get to work, get moving, Varta is a brand of batteries, same as *ponéte las pilas* (*pilas* means

batteries, thus the interchange with the brand name).

**ponerse media pila:** 1) to hurry up, go, get moving. 2) to cheer up, don't be depressed. 3) to stop being stupid. 4) to do something I want you to do.

**por dos mangos:** very cheap. *Compré estos collares por dos mangos.*

★ **por favor:** Argentines use this phrase, which normally means please in Spanish, as your welcome. It is used instead of the more common *de nada* in other countries. *¡Gracias! Por favor, no hay porqué.*

• **ponerse las pilas** •

★ **porfi:** short for *por favor*, please. *¿Me convidás un cigarrillo, porfi?*

💣 **poronga:** dick.

🍴 **pororó:** popcorn.

**porro:** a marijuana joint.

**portarse:** to do more than someone expected from you. *Se re portó mi suegra cuidando a los chicos todo el finde.*

★ **porteño:** a resident of Buenos Aires. *Soy cien por ciento porteño.*

**posta:** 1) genuine, not fake, for real, used as a noun or an interjection in the middle of a statement meaning that you are not bullshitting or that something difficult to believe is true. 2) excellent, magnificent.

🍴 **postre vigilante:** a dessert of pieces of cheese and quince paste.

**potro:** an attractive guy.

**pouch:** pronounced "poach" this word is used in reference to any type of small sample size package, for example with shampoos.

**precisar:** to need.

**prendió el ventilador:** to spill the beans, to tell it all.

**profanador de cunas:** a cradle robber, someone that dates much younger than their own age.

★ **prolijo:** correct, orderly, well done, proper. *Es muy prolijo en su trabajo y se destaca por su claridad.*

**prometer el oro y el moro:** to make all sorts of promises usually without fulfilling them.

**prontuario:** police record.

🍴 **provoleta:** a melted cheese appetizer with spices and sometimes sausage or bell peppers on top, often grilled.

**pucha:** shucks, darn, damn. *¡La gran pucha!*

🍴 **puchero:** a casserole.

★ **pucho:** a cigarette. *Apagá el pucho que viene el bondi.*

**puenting:** bungee jumping from a bridge.

**punga:** a pick-pocket.

**pura espuma:** all bark and no bite. *SYN:* puro bla bla.

**puro bla bla:** full of hot air, all bark and no bite. *Este tipo*

# puro chamuyo

es **puro bla bla**, yo no le creo nada. SYN: pura espuma.

★ **puro chamuyo:** complete lies. Te mandó **puro chamuyo**. No vendió ni la mitad de lo que te dijo, te lo aseguro.

**purrete:** a kid.

★ **¡que bajón!:** What a shame! What a pity! How depressing! **Qué bajón**, me afanaron el celu nuevo.

**¡qué choto!:** 1) What a fake! SYN: ¡Qué trucho! 2) What an asshole! SYN: ¡Qué boludo!

★ **¡que embole!:** 1) Boring! Vi una peli **que era un embole**, me quedé dormida en la mitad. 2) How annoying!, used when something annoying happens. Se me rompió una uña. **¡Qué embole!**

**¡qué flash!:** That's amazing!

**¡qué garcha!:** That sucks! Oh shit!

**¡que garrón!:** What a shame! What a pity!

**¡que grande!:** 1) You rock! Good to hear that! Congrats! 2) That's amazing, that's huge!, Holy Cow!

★ **¿que hacés?:** what's up?, what's going on?, a phrase

used to greet someone. Hola, Tere, **¿qué hacés?** ¿Todo bien?

★ **¡que malaria!:** unlucky, down on your luck. No tengo un mango, ¿y vos? Tampoco? **¡Qué malaria!**

**¡que me la chupe!:** I don't care what they say, screw them all!

★ **¿qué onda?:** 1) What are you up to?, What's going on? 2) What shall we do? 3) What's the deal? 4) What is it like? How do you like it?

**¡que percha!:** comment highlighting that because of the person's nice body any type of clothes look good. Lo lindo no es el vestido sino la **percha**.

**¡qué tarro!:** That was lucky!

★ **¿que te iba a decir?:** a common phrase used as a space filler in conversations. **¿Qué te iba a decir?** Así que te llamó y no lo atendiste.

★ **quedarse en bolas:** to be left without.

**quedarse en el molde:** to be quiet, relaxed.

**quedarse mosca:** to remain quiet, still.

**quedarse piola:** to stay cool, stay calm, to chill.

**quemarse:** to be ashamed or embarrassed.

**quemarse con leche:** comes from the saying *el que se quema con leche cuando ve una vaca llorar*, means once bitten twice shy.

**quemarse las pestañas:** to get down to it, to hit the books, to get to work.

**querer la chancha, los veinte y la máquina de hacer chorizos:** to have your cake and eat it too.

★ **¿Querés?:** Is that okay?

★ **querido / querida:** often used in an ironic sense to express that you are annoyed with or bugged by someone.

**quichicientas veces:** a million times, used in exaggeration meaning a whole lot.

**quien te quita lo bailado:** everything came out poorly, but at least you tried.

★ **quincho:** 1) a small building used for gatherings and BBQs, often at a vacation or weekend home. *Se vende casaquinta. Hermoso quincho* al fondo con parrilla y baño. 2) a toupee, rug. *El padre de Beti usa quincho, qué gracioso.*

**quinotos:** a guy's balls, nuts.

★ **quinta:** a property or retreat outside the city used for weekend and vacation getaways. *Tenemos una quinta en Pilar. Pasamos todos los fines de semana allá, salvo cuando llueve.*

🍴 **raba:** calamari, the more common Spanish word is also *calamari*.

★ **radiotaxi:** a special taxi generally called by telephone. *¿Tenés algún número de radiotaxi? Sino, me tomo uno en la calle pero a esta hora me da miedo.*

**rajar:** 1) to get out of Dodge, to leave immediately. 2) to throw someone out, to fire.

**rancho:** a small, shabby house, often used in reference to your own house.

**rasca:** 1) in poor taste, low class. 2) a stingy person.

**rata / ratón:** stingy, cheap.

**ratearse:** to skip school. *SYN:* hacerse la rata.

**rati:** police officer.

**raviol:** a gram of cocaine.

**rayado:** nuts, crazy.

★ **re:** prefix used to put emphasis on a word, for example *re-copado* means extremely cool.

**re pata:** a friendly, helpful person that asks for nothing in return.

**rea:** a dirty, low class woman.

**rebuscar:** to scrape by, to hustle to make a living, do lots of small jobs to make enough money to live.

**recién:** 1) to just have done something. *Recién llego a casa.* 2) not until. *Recién a las once llego a casa.*

**refregar:** to go at it sexually with someone (especially in public), to make out.

**regalada:** a woman who is ready to go sexually, there's no need to convince her.

**relojear:** to observe.

**remarla:** to make an effort.

★ **remise:** a type of taxi that has a fixed rate and is for longer trips, generally between different areas of a city. Sometimes regular taxis will not make these trips because they may not know the area, or, for the return part of the trip they will not have a fare. *Acá en el gran Buenos Aires casi no hay taxis. Tomate un **remise**. Tenés que llamarlo desde casa. No circulan como los taxis.*

🍴 **remolacha:** beet, another Spanish word is *betarraga*.

**reo:** 1) homeless. 2) scruffy. 3) carefree.

**repartija:** the splitting up of stolen goods.

**rescatarse:** to start leading a healthier life, usually clean from drugs.

**retobarse:** to rebel.

**revolear la carterita:** to be slutty. *Trola que anda **revoleando la cartera** de noche y de día se hace la lady.*

**rico guacho:** a hot guy.

🍴 **ristreto:** a small, extremely concentrated coffee, more concentrated than espresso.

**rompebolas:** pain in the ass, annoying.

**romper los quinotos:** to break someone's balls, bother someone.

**romperse el culo:** to work your ass off.

**romperse el orto:** to work your ass off.

**roña:** dirt, filth. *Qué roña que tengo, es hora de bañarse.*

**rope:** dog, the inverse of *perro*.

**sabiola:** a head.

**sacar cagando:** to cut off, to stop in one's tracks, to put a quick end to, to reject.

**sacar cuero:** to talk bad about someone.

**sacar la roja:** literally "to pull out the red", to warn or reprimand someone that does something wrong, comes from a receiving red card in soccer for a severe penalty. *Me **sacó** la roja la profe, se re dio cuenta que me estaba copiando en el examen.*

**sacar los garfios:** to get your hands off.

**sacarla barata:** to get away with something, the consequences could have been a lot worse.

**salame:** an idiot, fool.

**salamín:** a fool.

**salir a los piques:** to run away, leave in a hurry, to escape. *SYN:* salir picando.

**salir de levante:** to go out with the intention of picking up a girl or a guy. *Basta de sequía, **salgamos de levante**.*

**salir de trampa:** go out with the guys to look for chicks.

**salir en un pedo:** to head out quickly.

**salir picando:** to run away, leave in a hurry, to escape. *SYN:* salir a los piques.

🍴 **salsa criolla:** a sauce of chopped red bell pepper, onion and vinegar used to put on top of beef.

🍴 **salsa rosada:** a pasta sauce that is a mix of tomato sauce and alfredo sauce, thus the name *salsa rosada* ("pink sauce" in Spanish).

**sanata:** to lie, make things up, to smooth talk.

🍴 **scarparo:** pasta sauce with tomato, olive oil, garlic, basil, and cream.

💣 **se la come:** a queer, a fag.

**seca:** a puff of a cigarette.

# seco

**seco:** indigent, poor.

**seguíme, chango:** follow me.

**segurola:** sure.

**sentar cabeza:** to settle down, have a family.

**ser boleta:** 1) to die. 2) to suffer the consequences.

**ser de fierro:** 1) solid as a rock, well-made. 2) trustworthy. *Sos un amigo de fierro, hermano.*

**ser de madera:** to be bad at something. *SYN:* ser un queso.

**ser dejado en banda:** be stood up, left waiting.

**ser del palo:** part of the group.

**ser el hijo del vidriero:** phrase used to tell someone that they are blocking one's vision, you make a better door than a window. *Corréte que no veo. ¿Quién sos? ¿El hijo del vidriero?*

**ser hijo del sodero / del lechero:** said of a child that does not resemble his / her father, the milkman's child.

**ser ni chicha ni limonada:** in the middle, undecided.

**ser un bala:** queer, gay, a fag.

**ser un cabeza:** sleazy.

**ser un colgado:** be someone who leaves people hanging, doesn't keep his / her word (in meetings with people, etc.). *No seas colgado y llamame para mi cumpleaños.*

**ser un colgueti:** see *ser un colgado.*

**ser un despiste:** to be scatter-brained.

**ser un mandado:** to be a risk-taker in a reckless way.

**ser un nono, estar nono:** to behave like and old person, mainly when a person doesn't feel like going out.

**ser un pirata:** a guy who goes out with a lot of women and never gets involved.

**ser un queso:** to be bad at something. *Maria es un queso bailando. SYN:* ser de madera.

**ser un tiro al aire:** to be carefree.

**ser un versero:** someone that speaks eloquently but really does not know what he is saying, talking through your nose.

**ser yeta:** a jinx, a person that brings bad luck.

**serruchar el piso:** try to get what someone has usually through bad behavior.

**service:** service, attention.

**shopping:** a mall. *Fuimos a ese shopping enorme sobre la Panamericana que se llama Unicenter para encontrar todas las tiendas interesantes.*

★ **sí o sí:** literally "yes or yes", definitely, it must happen, it will happen no matter what. *Voy sí o sí, no me pierdo el show ni que venga el Papa.*

**sin pena ni gloria:** almost unnoticed.

**siome:** fool, idiot. *SYN:* boludo, tarado.

**si te digo que es carnaval vos apretá el pomo:** listen to me, I know what I'm talking about. *SYN:* ponéle la firma.

**sobrador:** someone who acts with arrogance.

**sobrar:** to belittle someone, to act superior to.

**sobre:** a bed.

**sobre el pucho:** last minute.

**socotroco:** a big piece of something of uncomfortable, awkward shape.

**soda:** carbonated water.

**sodero:** a person that goes door to door delivering carbonated bottled water.

**solari:** to be alone. *Me fui de vacaciones solari.*

**sommier:** a box spring for a bed.

**sonar:** 1) to die. 2) to be screwed up, crazy.

• si te digo que es carnaval vos apretá el pomo •

**sopapo:** a face slap.

**sorete:** 1) a turd (the actual, physical thing). 2) a turd (as in an annoying, shitty person).

**sorrentino:** a large ravioli-like type of pasta.

# MONEY

*Loot, moolah, bucks, dough, greenbacks, dead presidents, sawbacks, cash, dinero, smackaroos, greasing a palm...here's how to say it in Argentina.*

**amarrete:** cheap, stingy.
**amarrocar:** to save money
**austral:** name of former currency used in Argentina, replaced by the peso in 1992
**bono:** any of a number of different currencies emitted by the various provinces of Argentina as an attempt to stabilize their fiscal problems. Although the word literally means bond, they were in effect currencies printed to pay off debt.
**chirola:** coins, pocket change
**cobre:** money
**coima:** a bribe
**coimear:** to bribe
**cometa:** a bribe
**corralito:** word used to describe the step the government took in 2001 and 2002 to seize bank deposits and control the amount of money people could withdraw from their accounts
**gamba:** one hundred pesos
**gatillar:** to spend a lot of money
**guita:** bucks, money
**luca:** one thousand of a currency, one *luca* is a thousand dollars or pesos
**luca verde:** a thousand US dollars
**mango:** 1) money  2) very little or none (in reference to money)
**morlaco:** money
**mosca:** money
**palo:** a million
**palo verde:** a million dollars

**sorullo:** a turd.

**sos boleta:** you're dead, they're gonna kill you.

**¿sos o te hacés?:** Are you actually stupid or just acting?

**sos un fenómeno:** You are great! You are cool! *¡Sos un fenómeno, flaco! ¡Un groso!*

● **sos un sorete:** You're a piece of shit!, a liar, a turd.

● **sos un sorongo:** same as *sos un sorete.*

● **sos un sorullo:** You're a piece of shit!, a liar, a turd.

**su gracia:** another way of asking your name.

**subirle la tanada:** to get furious, in a loud, aggressive, or destructive manner.

[♨] **submarino:** hot milk served with a piece of chocolate melting inside.

**sucucho:** any small place or room.

**sudar la gota gorda:** to suffer to the very end.

**suertudo:** someone lucky or fortunate.

[♨] **suprema napolitana:** a *milanesa* with melted cheese and tomato sauce on top.

**tachero:** a taxi driver.

**tamangos:** rustic shoes.

**tanga:** a g-string.

**tanito castigador:** someone that gets a lot of women, often in reference to an Italian or someone of Italian heritage.

**tano:** any Italian.

**tanque (australiano):** a fat or obese person.

★ **tarado:** idiot.

● **taradúpido:** a mix between *tarado* and *estúpido*, something along the lines of a dumbass. *SYN:* tarúpido.

**tardar un huevo:** to take a long time.

**tarro:** luck.

[♨] **tarta:** quiche.

**tarúpido:** a combination of the words *tarado* and *estúpido*, a really stupid idiot, an extremely dumb person. *¡Cállate **tarúpido**, infeliz, nabo!. SYN:* taradúpido.

**taxiboy:** a male prostitute.

**te cortaron verde:** immature.

# te piraste mal

**te piraste mal:** to leave.

**telo:** The inverse of the word hotel, but refers more specifically when used for sexual encounters. Rooms are generally rented by the hour, for short-term occupation. *Ya que los chicos viven con los padres tienen sexo en un **telo**. ¡No les queda otra!*

**tener (un) orto:** to have a lot of luck. *SYN:* tener culo.

**tener arrastre:** to be sexually appealing. *Qué suerte que tiene! **Tiene un arrastre** bárbaro. Nunca le falta un candidato. SYN:* tener levante.

**tener asfalto:** to have experience. *SYN:* tener calle.

★ **tener calle:** to have experience. ***Tiene mucha calle**. Imagínate que vive solo desde los 15 años, cuando lo emanciparon sus padres.*

**tener chucho:** to be afraid.

**tener de hijo:** means to totally dominate, for example one sports team over another.

**tener hasta la coronilla:** to be fed up with.

**tener junado:** to know someone, to know what they're really like, to read them like a book.

**tener la manija:** to have things under control.

**tener la posta:** to be sure, to have precise information nobody else has.

**tener las bolas llenas:** to be fed up with.

• **tener las bolas por el piso** •

**tener las bolas por el piso:** to be fed up with.

★ **tener labia:** to have the ability to speak eloquently, convince people by talking to them. ***Tiene labia**. Se parla a los profesores y consigue lo que quiere.*

**tener mala pata:** to be unlucky.

**tener menos calle que Venecia:** to not have experience, to not be street-wise.

**tener pila de ganas:** to have a lot of desire to do something.

💣 **tener un afrecho:** to fuck.

**tener un cocodrilo en el bolsillo:** to be cheap, stingy.

**tener un filito:** to have a companion, someone to go out with, hang out with, always in a romantic sense.

**tener un metejón:** to be in love.

★ **tener un pedo bárbaro:** to be really drunk.

**tener una vena:** to be angry, pissed off or frustrated. *SYN:* tener bronca.

**tener verso:** to have the ability to speak eloquently.

**tenerla clara:** to know something well, to have a deep knowledge of something.

**tenerla muerta:** completely in love with.

**tilinga:** low-class, a street person.

**timba:** gambling.

**timbear:** to gamble.

**timbero:** a gambler.

🍴 **tintillo:** red wine.

★ **tipo:** a sentence filler, similar to "like" in English.

**tirar a la marchanta:** to throw in the air for people to catch what is being given away (for example, candy at a birthday party). *Es típico que en los cumpleaños **se tiren caramelos a la marchanta**.*

**tirar la chancleta:** to be slutty. *Se cansó de tantos años de desgraciado matrimonio y tiró la chancleta.*

**tirar la goma:** to masturbate, literally ¨to pull the rubber¨.

**tirar la toalla:** to give up, surrender.

**tirar los galgos:** to hit on, to try to pick up, to make a pass at.

**tirar manteca al techo:** to have a lot of something. *No estamos como para **tirar manteca al techo** pero se recompuso bastante la economía en el hogar.*

# tirar una bomba

**tirar una bomba:** to reveal some surprising or scandalous news (both negative and positive). *Mi hermana tiró a la familia una bomba cuando anunció que está embarazada, pero no sabe quien es el papá.*

**tirar una cana al aire:** to be unfaithful.

**tirar una soga:** to help out, to lend a hand.

**tirarme las agujas:** phrase used for What time is it?, literally "throw me the needles".

**tiro al aire:** carefree.

**toga:** cat, the inverse of *gato*.

**toletole:** a mess, a screw-up.

**tomado:** drunk.

[🍽] **tomarse un vinasi:** to have a drink of wine.

**tordo:** a doctor, refers to a lawyer or medical doctor, inverse of *doctor*. *¿Cómo le va, tordo? Dígame qué tengo; me siento mal, pero muy mal.*

💣 **toronjas:** boobs, tits.

💣 **torta:** a lesbian.

💣 **tortillera:** lesbian.

**tortolito:** infatuated, in love.

[🍽] **tostado mixto:** a toasted ham and cheese sandwich on bread.

**traba:** transvestite.

**trabucarse:** to get stuck.

**trabuco:** transvestite.

**trajeado:** dressed up, literally "suited".

**tranca:** relaxed, laid back, comes from *tranquilo*.

★ **tranqui:** tranquil, relaxed, chilling. *Tranqui, no te pongas nervioso que es sólo una entrevista.*

★ 💣 **transar:** 1) to make out, to fool around. *Me transé a la novia de mi amigo.* 2) to be messing around with someone, no strings attached. *No estamos de novios. Estamos transando.* 3) to compromise on something. 4) to deal drugs. *Hizo su fortuna transando con el gobierno de turno.*

**tránsfuga:** someone without morals.

**tranzar:** alternate spelling of *transar*.

★ **trasnochar:** to stay out all night partying, arriving home

**104**

after the sun comes up. *Ayer trasnoché y hoy me desperté re temprano con la obra en construcción en frente de casa.*

**traste:** rear end, heinie.

**traviesa:** transvestite.

**trepador:** someone that climbs over people or steps on people to advance their own interests (ex. in the office)

💣 **trolo:** a queer, a fag.

**trompa:** boss, owner, inverse of *patrón*.

**trompear:** to beat someone. *SYN:* fajar.

**tronco:** clumsy.

★ **trucho:** false, fake, bogus. *Alquilé un DVD truchísimo, re pirata.*

**truco:** a game of cards specific to Argentina.

**tubo:** telephone.

🍴 **tuco:** tomato sauce.

**tumba:** prison.

💣 **turca:** jerk off with a woman's tits.

**turradas:** stupidities, evil or annoying actions that make

others suffer. *Las **turradas** del gobierno están tirando al país al tacho. SYN:* guachada.

**turro/a:** a son of a bitch, a mean, bad person, an asshole. *El **turro** de mi jefe no me da permiso ni para ir al médico.*

**¡Ufa!:** darn, shucks. *¡Ufa!, tenía unas ganas de ir al cine con vos. Que pena que no podés.*

**un agreta:** bitter, detached.

**un caño:** something or someone fabulous, amazing.

**un fato:** a fling.

**un garca:** a con man, a fraud.

**un huesito:** a fling. *SYN:* un fato.

★ **un huevo:** a lot of something. *Me costó **un huevo** y medio entender el problema.*

**un kilo y dos pancitos:** to be okay, to be all right.

**un pelo de concha tira más que 100 bueyes:** describes when a man is dating someone and ignores his friends, stops going out with them to be with his girlfriend.

**un pichi:** an inexperienced person, a new business, espe-

# un polvo no se le niega a nadie

cially when compared to more experienced ones.

★ 💣 **un polvo no se le niega a nadie:** used to express that having sex with the person is something momentary, or not a serious relationship, literally "a fuck is not denied to anyone". *Me tiró onda, a mí no me gusta mucho pero bueno,* **un polvo no se le niega a nadie**.

**un vagón:** 1) a beautiful woman, a hot babe or chick. *SYN:* un camión. 2) a lot of something. *Me compré* **un vagón** *de ropa en oferta ayer.*

**una máquina:** a car or computer or some device that works very well.

**una paquetería:** something refined.

**vacana:** someone that enjoys the good life.

**vagoneta:** lazy, vagrant.

**vamo y vamo (vamos y vamos):** fifty-fifty, split down the middle.

**vender hasta a la madre:** completely unscrupulous, literally "to sell even one's mother"

• **venderle un buzón** •

**venderle un buzón:** to cheat someone, pull the wool over their eyes, to sell someone the Brooklyn Bridge. *Voy a averiguar sobre los componentes de la máquina. A mi no me van a* **vender un buzón**.

**ventajear:** to put oneself in an advantageous position by cheating.

**ventilador:** a fan (ex. ceiling fan).

**verde:** a person, joke or comment with a sexual connotation.

**verduguear:** to treat someone badly or poorly, humiliate.

**versear:** to make up, lie.

# CRIME

**afanar:** to steal, rob or swindle
**arbolito:** an illegal money changer (the changing of money is controlled by the government)
**batidor:** a snitch, informant
**bocina:** a snitch
**bocón:** a snitch
**boga:** lawyer
**botón:** 1) a police officer  2) a snitch
**botonazo:** a snitch
**botonear:** to inform on, give someone away, betray
**buchón:** a snitch, informant
**buchonear:** to inform, give someone away, betray
**cachiporra:** a police night stick
**campana:** a lookout during a robbery
**cana:** the police
**chorear:** to steal
**chorro:** a dirty, rotten thief
**cobanis:** police officers as referred to by thieves
**curro:** 1) a thief  2) small job
**dechavar / deschavar:** to snitch on, denounce
**estar en cana:** to be in jail, prison
**estar guardado:** to be in jail
**falopa:** drugs
**falopearse:** to shoot up, use drugs
**falopero:** a drug addict
**garca:** a swindler, a cheater, the inverse of *cagar*
**gato:** a prostitute
**guardado:** imprisoned
**prontuario:** police record
**punga:** a pick-pocket
**rati:** police officer
**tumba:** prison
**vigilante:** 1) an informant, a snitch  2) a police officer
**yuta:** a police officer

# versero

**versero:** 1) a pick-up artist. 2) someone that talks as if he / she is well-versed in a topic, but is actually making it up or lying.

**vichar:** to spy.

★ **viejo/a:** dad or mom, an affectionate term for one's parents. *Anoche mis **viejos** salieron a cenar en Recoleta con unos amigos.*

**vigilante:** 1) an informant, a snitch. 2) a type of pastry. 3) a police officer.

**villa miseria:** a slum area, often controlled by criminals.

🍴 **vinacho:** wine.

**viola:** a guitar.

★ **¿Viste?:** this is a filler word that has no particular meaning, similar to "you know" or "like" in English. *¿**Viste?** Qué te dije que iba a llegar a las 6 en punto.*

**viva la pepa:** on the loose, wild, wacky, crazy. *Cuando la maestra sale un minuto, la sala es un **viva la pepa**.*

**volver con la cola entre las patas:** to be afraid or ashamed of someone's reaction for having done some-

thing bad.

**winner:** a guy that gets a lot of women.

**ya fue:** it's in the past, there's nothing you can do now, it's water under the bridge, forget about it.

★ **yanqui:** 1) an American. *Tengo varios amigos **yanquis**.* 2) anything related to American culture. *Esa gorra es re **yanqui**, parecés un jugador de béisbol.*

**yeca:** experience, the inverse of *calle*, literally "street" as in street smarts.

**yegua:** someone that gets involved in petty bitching, arguing and complaining (most often used in reference to women).

★ 💣 **yerba:** 1) the tea that is used in drinking mate. 2) weed, marijuana.

**yeta:** a jinx, a person that brings bad luck.

**yirar:** to walk or wander.

💣 **yiro:** a slut, whore.

**yugar:** to work hard.

**yugo:** work, job. *Y bueno, terminaron las vacaciones, de* *vuelta al **yugo.***

**¡yupi!:** Yipee! Yahoo! Yee-haw!

**yuta:** a police officer.

★ **zafar:** 1) to get out of or escape from a sticky situation. *No estaba preparado para mi examen, pero **zafé** porque sonó la alarma de incendio en el edificio.* 2) to squeak by. *Pedro **zafó** con el mínimo aceptable para entrar a la facu.*

**zamarear:** to shake (a child).

**zampar:** to beat, hit.

**zapallo:** a fool.

**zapán:** tummy, the inverse of *panza.*

**zaparrastrozo:** a run-down looking person.

**zapping:** channel surfing. *Anoche no hice nada, me tomé una cervecita y me quedé haciendo **zapping.***

**zarpado:** 1) a nut job, or crazy person, that does something inappropriate or out of place for the setting, someone that crosses the line. 2) cool, awesome, great.

**zurdo:** a leftist, communist.

# About the Author

Photo Credit:
Diana Caballero, 2008.

**S**uffering a typical 9-5 existence, Jared's foray into lunch-hour Spanish shook up his mundane life. He quit his job, stopped by briefly to school, and then left his country...for 14 years. Early stumblings in real-world Spanish taught him that a *cola* isn't just a soft drink, *bicho* doesn't always mean a bug, and *boludo* may be heartfelt or middle-finger felt. Nine countries, three business start-ups, two bestsellers and a Puerto Rican wife later, he is still confounded by how many Spanish words exist for panties. His quest is to discover all those words. In between, he meanders the Earth, dabbles in languages, drinks wine and sells shampoo.

**S**ufriendo la típica vida corporativa de 9am a 5pm, la incursión de Jared en el español durante sus horas de almuerzo le dieron un giro a su vida común. Dejó su empleo, realizó estudios y luego abandonó su país... por 14 años. Sus inicios con el español del mundo real le enseñaron que la *cola* no es sólo una bebida carbonatada, que *bicho* no siempre significa un insecto y que *boludo* puede tener una connotación cordial y también insultante. Después de una trayectoria de nueve países, tres empresas fundadas, dos libros en las listas de los más vendidos y una esposa puertorriqueña, Jared sigue confundido por la cantidad de palabras que existen en español para *panties*. Su meta es descubrir todas esas palabras. Mientras tanto, él pasea por el mundo, coquetea con los idiomas, bebe vino y vende champú.

Any comments, corrections or inclusions should be sent to
*Pueden enviar cualquier comentario, corrección o sugerencia a*
**info@SpeakingLatino.com**

Books from Jared Romey's Speaking Latino series
*Libros de la serie Speaking Latino de Jared Romey*

**Speaking Boricua**
A Practical Guide to
Puerto Rican Spanish

**Speaking Phrases Boricua**
A Collection of Wisdom and
Sayings from Puerto Rico

**Speaking Argento**
A Guide to Argentine Spanish

**Speaking Chileno**
A Guide to Chilean Slang

Follow Speaking Latino and Jared Romey
*Sigue a Speaking Latino y a Jared Romey*

**Páginas Facebook**
Speaking Latino
Jared Romey

**Twitter**
@jaredromey

**Google +**
Speaking Latino

**Speaking Latino Website & Blog**
Search the FREE database with more than 8,000 slang words and phrases from Latin
America at www.SpeakingLatino.com
***Página de Internet & Blog de Speaking Latino***
*Consulta GRATIS la base de datos con más de 8,000 palabras y frases de jerga Latino-
americana en www.SpeakingLatino.com*